P9-DBS-847

BLESSINGS
for **Women** *and* PRAYERS

A DEVOTIONAL COMPANION

CONCORDIA PUBLISHING HOUSE · SAINT LOUIS

Contents

Prayer is a natural and common part of the Christian's conversation with God; a conversation He initiates in Word and Sacrament. The prayer of a Christian flows from the relationship forged by the Savior who, by His sacrifice on the cross, has given you access to the heart of God. Prayer is not merely a pious act, but a way to bring glory to God and tend to your and your neighbor's bodily and spiritual welfare.

The prayers, meditations, and verses included in this collection have been in use in the church for many years. The goal of this little book is to be a convenient resource to inform and encourage you in your prayer life.

The familiar words and rhythms selected for this devotional are drawn from the words often heard in worship as we gather in community. Through regular use they can assist you in making your whole life one of communion with your gracious heavenly Father.

Editor

Let the words of my mouth and
the meditation of my heart

be acceptable in Your sight,
O Lord, my Rock and my Redeemer.

Psalm 19:14

For Individuals and Small Groups

These brief services are intended as a simple form of daily prayer for individuals, families, small groups, and other settings.

When more than one person is present, the versicles and responses may be spoken responsively, with one person reading the words in regular type and the others responding with the words in bold type. Prayers may be prayed in the same fashion, though those in bold type are to be prayed by all.

For the readings, several verses have been recommended for each particular time of day. These may be used on a rotating basis. The value in using these few texts lies in the opportunity to learn them well. For those desiring a more complete selection of readings, daily lectionaries, such as those found in a hymnal may be used. Meditations as well as readings from Luther's Small and Large Catechisms may be included.

In the "prayers for others and ourselves," the following suggestions are intended to establish a pattern of daily and weekly prayer.

Sunday: For the joy of the resurrection among us; for the fruit of faith nourished by the Word and the Sacraments.

Monday: For faith to live in the promises of Holy Baptism; for one's calling and daily work; for the unemployed; for the salvation and well-being of our neighbors; for schools, colleges, and seminaries; for good government and for peace.

Tuesday: For deliverance against temptation and evil; for the addicted and despairing, the tortured and oppressed; for those struggling with sin.

Wednesday: For marriage and family, that husbands and wives, parents and children live in ordered harmony according to the Word of God; for parents who must raise children alone; for those looking for a faithful spouse; for our communities and neighborhoods.

Thursday: For the Church and her pastors; for teachers, deacons and deaconesses, for missionaries, and for all who serve the Church; for fruitful and salutary use of the blessed Sacrament of Christ's body and blood.

Friday: For the preaching of the holy cross of our Lord Jesus Christ and for the spread of His knowledge throughout the whole world; for the persecuted and oppressed; for the sick and dying.

Saturday: For faithfulness to the end; for the renewal of those who are withering in the faith or have fallen away; for receptive hearts and minds to God's Word on the Lord's Day; for pastors and people as they prepare to administer and receive Christ's holy gifts.

The sign of the cross may be made by all in remembrance of their Baptism.

In the name of the Father and of the ✠ Son and of the Holy Spirit.

Amen.
O Lord, in the morning you hear my voice;
in the morning I prepare a sacrifice for you and watch. *Psalm 5:3*
My mouth is filled with Your praise,
and with your glory all the day. *Psalm 71:8*
O Lord, open my lips,
and my mouth will declare your praise.
Psalm 51:15
Glory be to the Father and to the Son and to the Holy Spirit; as it was in the beginning, is now, and will be forever. Amen.

A hymn, canticle, or psalm may be sung or spoken. An appointed reading or one of the following is read: Colossians 3:1–4; Exodus 15:1–11; Isaiah 12:1–6; Matthew 20:1–16; Mark 13:32–36; Luke 24:1–8; John 21:4–14; Ephesians 4:17–24; Romans 6:1–4.

A meditation or selection from the catechism may be read.

The Apostles' Creed is confessed.
Lord's Prayer
Prayers for others and ourselves
Concluding prayers:

Almighty God, merciful Father, who created and completed all things, on this day when the work of our calling begins anew, we implore You to create its beginning, direct its continuance, and bless its end, that our doings may be preserved from sin, our life sanctified, and our work this day be well pleasing to You; through Jesus Christ, our Lord. **Amen**.

I thank You, my heavenly Father, through Jesus Christ, Your dear Son, that You have kept me this night from all harm and danger; and I pray that You would keep me this day also from sin and every evil, that all my doings and life may please You. For into Your hands I commend myself, my body and soul, and all things. Let Your holy angel be with me, that the evil foe may have no power over me. Amen. (Luther's Morning Prayer, Small Catechism)

Let us bless the Lord.
Thanks be to God.
Then go joyfully to your work.

12

The sign of the cross may be made by all in remembrance of their Baptism.

In the name of the Father and of the ✠ Son and of the Holy Spirit.

Amen.
Listen to my prayer, O God, do not ignore my plea;
hear my prayer and answer me.
Evening, morning, and noon
I cry out in distress and He hears my voice.
Cast your cares on the Lord and He will sustain you;
He will never let the righteous fall. *Psalm 55:1, 16–17, 22*
Glory be to the Father and to the Son and to the Holy Spirit; as it was in the beginning, is now, and will be forever. Amen.

A hymn, canticle, or psalm may be sung or said.
An appointed reading or one of the following is read:
1 Corinthians 7:17a, 23–24; Luke 23:44–46;
Matthew 5:13–16; Matthew 13:1–9, 18–23; Mark
13:23–27; John 15:1–9; Romans 7:18–25; Romans

12:1–2; 1 Peter 1:3–9.

O Lord,
have mercy upon us.
O Christ,
have mercy upon us.
O Lord,
have mercy upon us.

Lord's Prayer
Prayers for others and ourselves
Concluding prayer:
Blessed Lord Jesus Christ, at this hour You hung
upon the cross, stretching out Your loving arms
to embrace the world in Your death. Grant that
all people of the earth may look to You and see
their salvation; for your mercy's sake we pray.
Amen.
(OR)
Heavenly Father, send Your Holy Spirit into our
hearts, to direct and rule us according to Your
will, to comfort us in all our afflictions, to
defend us from all error, and to lead us into all
truth; through Jesus Christ, our Lord. **Amen**.

Let us bless the Lord.
Thanks be to God.

The sign of the cross may be made by all in remembrance of their Baptism.

In the name of the Father and of the ✠ Son and of the Holy Spirit.

Amen.
A candle may be lighted.
Let my prayer rise before You as incense;

the lifting up of my hands as the evening sacrifice.   *Psalm 141:2*

Joyous light of glory of the immortal Father; heavenly, holy, blessed Jesus Christ. We have come to the setting of the sun, and we look to the evening light. We sing to God, the Father, Son, and Holy Spirit: You are worthy of being praised with pure voices forever. O Son of God, O giver of life: the universe proclaims Your glory.

A hymn, canticle, or psalm may be sung or said.
An appointed reading or one of the following is read:
Luke 24:28–31; Exodus 16:11–21, 31; Isaiah 25:6–9; Matthew 14:15–21; Matthew 27:57–60; Luke 14:15–24; John 6:25–35; John 10:7–18; Ephesians 6:10–18.

A meditation or selection from the catechism may be read.

Lord's Prayer
Prayers for others and ourselves
Concluding prayer:
Lord Jesus, stay with us, for the evening is at hand and the day is past. Be our constant companion on the way, kindle our hearts, and awaken hope among us, that we may recognize You as You are revealed in the Scriptures and in the Breaking of the Bread. Grant this for Your name's sake. **Amen.**

Let us bless the Lord.

Thanks be to God.

Mealtime Prayers:

Asking a blessing before the meal
Lord God, heavenly Father, bless us and these Your gifts which we receive from Your bountiful goodness, through Jesus Christ, our Lord. Amen.

Returning thanks after the meal
We thank You, Lord God, heavenly Father, through Jesus Christ, our Lord, for all Your benefits, who lives and reigns with You forever and ever. Amen.

The sign of the cross may be made by all in remembrance of their Baptism.

In the name of the Father and of the ✠ Son and of the Holy Spirit.
Amen.
The Lord Almighty grant us a quiet night and peace at the last.
Amen.
It is good to give thanks to the Lord,
to sing praise to Your name, O Most High;
To herald Your love in the morning,

Your truth at the close of the day.
An appointed reading or one of the following is read: Matthew 11:28–30; Micah 7:18–20; Matthew 18:15–35; Matthew 25:1–13; Luke 11:1–13; Luke 12:13–34; Romans 8:31–39; 2 Corinthians 4:16–18; Revelation 21:22–22:5.

The Apostles' Creed is confessed.
Lord, now You let Your servant go in peace;
Your word has been fulfilled.
My own eyes have seen the salvation

17

which You have prepared in the sight of every people:
a light to lighten the nations
and the glory of Your people Israel. *Luke 2:29–32*
Glory be to the Father and to the Son and to the Holy Spirit;
as it was in the beginning, is now, and will be forever. Amen.

Lord's Prayer
Prayers for others and ourselves
Concluding prayers:
Visit our dwellings, O Lord, and in Your great mercy defend us from all perils and dangers of this night; for the love of Your only Son, our Savior Jesus Christ. **Amen.**
I thank You, my heavenly Father, through Jesus Christ, Your dear Son, that You have graciously kept me this day; and I pray that You would forgive me all my sins where I have done wrong, and graciously keep me this night. For into Your hands I commend myself, my body and soul, and all things. Let Your holy angel be with me, that the evil foe may have no power over me. Amen.

(Luther's Evening Prayer, Small Catechism)

Let us bless the Lord.
Thanks be to God.
Then be at peace and rest in God's care.

Selection of Hymns

The following selected hymns are appropriate for the festivals of the church year:

Advent

Christmas

Lent

Easter

Trinity/Pentecost

Reformation

Thanksgiving

Baptism

A Mighty Fortress Is Our God

1. A mighty fortress is our God,
   A trusty Shield and Weapon;
   He helps us free from ev'ry need
   That hath us now o'ertaken.
   The old evil Foe
   Now means deadly woe;
   Deep guile and great might
   Are his dread arms in fight;
   On earth is not his equal.

2. With might of ours can naught be done,
   Soon were our loss effected;
   But for us fights the Valiant One,
   Whom God Himself elected.
   Ask ye, Who is this?
   Jesus Christ it is.
   Of Sabaoth Lord,
   And there's none other God;
   He holds the field forever.

3. Though devils all the world should fill,
   All eager to devour us,
   We tremble not, we fear no ill,
   They shall not overpower us.
   This world's prince may still
   Scowl fierce as he will,
   He can harm us none,
   He's judged; the deed is done;
   One little word can fell him.

4. The Word they still shall let remain
   Nor any thanks have for it;
   He's by our side upon the plain
   With His good gifts and Spirit.
   And take they our life,
   Goods, fame, child, and wife,
   Let these all be gone,
   They yet have nothing won;
   The Kingdom ours remaineth.

Text: Martin Luther, 1483–1546

Abide with Me

1. Abide with me, fast falls the eventide.
   The darkness deepens; Lord with me abide.
   When other helpers fail and comforts flee,
   Help of the helpless, oh, abide with me.

2. I need Thy presence every passing hour;
   What but Thy grace can foil the Tempter's
   power?
   Who like Thyself my guide and stay can be?
   Through cloud and sunshine, oh, abide with
   me.

3. Swift to its close ebbs out life's little day;
   Earth's joys grow dim, its glories pass away;
   Change and decay in all around I see.
   O Thou, who changest not, abide with me.

4. Thou on my head in early youth didst smile,
   And though rebellious and perverse mean-
   while,

Thou hast not left me, oft as I left Thee.
On to the close, O Lord, abide with me.

5. I fear no foe, with Thee at hand to bless;
Ills have no weight and tears no bitterness,
Where is death's sting? where, grave, thy victory?
I triumph still if Thou abide with me.

6. Hold Thou Thy cross before my closing eyes,
Shine through the gloom, and point me to
the skies.
Heaven's morning breaks, and earth's vain
shadows flee;
In life, in death, O Lord, abide with me.

Author: Henry F. Lyte, 1793–1847

Amazing Grace

1. Amazing grace! How sweet the sound
That saved a wretch like me!
I once was lost but now am found,
Was blind but now I see!

2. The Lord has promised good to me,
His word my hope secures;
He will my shield and portion be
As long as life endures.

3. Through many dangers, toils, and snares
I have already come;
His grace has brought me safe so far,
His grace will see me home.

4. Yes, when this flesh and heart shall fail

And mortal life shall cease,
Amazing grace shall then prevail
In heaven's joy and peace.

Text: John Newton, 1725–1807, alt.

Baptized into Your Name Most Holy

1. Baptized into your name most holy,
   O Father, Son, and Holy Ghost,
   I claim a place, though weak and lowly,
   Among your seed, your chosen host.
   Buried with Christ and dead to sin,
   I have your Spirit now within.

2. My loving Father, here you take me
   Henceforth to be your child and heir;
   My faithful Savior, here you make me
   The fruit of all your sorrows share;
   O Holy Ghost, you comfort me
   Though threat'ning clouds around I see.

3. O faithful God, you never fail me;
   Your cov'nant surely will abide.
   Let not eternal death assail me
   Should I transgress it on my side!
   Have mercy when I come defiled;
   Forgive, lift up, restore your child.

4. All that I am and love most dearly,
   Receive it all, O Lord, from me.
   Oh, let me make my vows sincerely,
   And help me your own child to be!
   Let nothing that I am or own

Serve any will but yours alone.

Text: Johann J. Rambach, 1693–1735;
tr. Catherine Winkworth, 1829–78, alt.

Beautiful Savior

1. Beautiful Savior,
   King of creation,
   Son of God and Son of Man!
   Truly I'd love thee,
   Truly I'd serve thee,
   Light of my soul, my joy, my crown.

2. Fair are the meadows,
   Fair are the woodlands,
   Robed in flow'rs of blooming spring;
   Jesus is fairer,
   Jesus is purer,
   He makes our sorr'wing spirit sing.

3. Fair is the sunshine,
   Fair is the moonlight,
   Bright the sparkling stars on high;
   Jesus shines brighter,
   Jesus shines purer
   Than all the angels in the sky.

4. Beautiful Savior,
   Lord of the nations,
   Son of God and Son of Man!
   Glory and honor,
   Praise, adoration
   Now and forevermore be thine!

Text: Gesangbuch, Munster, 1677;
tr. Joseph A. Seiss, 1823–1904

Be Still, My Soul

1. Be still, my soul; the Lord is on your side;
   Bear patiently the cross of grief or pain;
   Leave to your God to order and provide;
   In every change he faithful will remain.
   Be still, my soul; your best, your heavenly Friend
   Through thorny ways leads to a joyful end.

2. Be still, my soul; your God will undertake
   To guide the future as he has the past.
   Your hope, your confidence let nothing shake;
   All now mysterious shall be bright at last.
   Be still, my soul; the waves and wind still know
   His voice who ruled them while he dwelt below.

3. Be still, my soul; though dearest friends depart
   And all is darkened in the vale of tears;
   Then you will better know his love, his heart,
   Who comes to soothe your sorrows and your
       fears.
   Be still, my soul; your Jesus can repay
   From his own fullness all he takes away.

4. Be still, my soul; the hour is hastening on
   When we shall be forever with the Lord,
   When disappointment, grief, and fear are gone,
   Sorrow forgot, love's purest joys restored.
   Be still, my soul; when change and tears
       are past,
   All safe and blessed we shall meet at last.

Text: Catharina von Schlegel, b. 1697;
tr. Jane Borthwick, 1813–97, alt.

Blest Be the Tie That Binds

1. Blest be the tie that binds
   Our hearts in Christian love;
   The unity of heart and mind
   Is like to that above.

2. Before our Father's throne
   We pour our ardent prayers;
   Our fears, our hopes, our aims are one,
   Our comforts and our cares.

3. We share our mutual woes,
   Our mutual burdens bear,
   And often for each other flows
   The sympathizing tear.

4. From sorrow, toil, and pain
   And sin we shall be free,
   And perfect love and friendship reign
   Through all eternity.

Text: Lowell Mason

Chief of Sinners Though I Be

1. Chief of sinners though I be,
   Jesus shed his blood for me,
   Died that I might live on high,
   Lives that I might never die.
   As the branch is to the vine,
   I am his, and he is mine.

2. Oh, the height of Jesus' love,
   Higher than the heav'ns above,

29

Deeper than the depths of sea,
Lasting as eternity!
Love that found me—wondrous thought—
Found me when I sought him not.

3. Only Jesus can impart
   Balm to heal the wounded heart,
   Peace that flows from sin forgiv'n,
   Joy that lifts the soul to heav'n,
   Faith and hope to walk with God
   In the way that Enoch trod.

4. Chief of sinners though I be,
   Christ is all in all to me;
   All my wants to him are known,
   All my sorrows are his own.
   He sustains the hidden life
   Safe with him from earthly strife.

5. O my Savior, help afford
   By your Spirit and your Word!
   When my wayward heart would stray,
   Keep me in the narrow way;
   Grace in time of need supply
   While I live and when I die.

Text: Richard Redhead

Christ, the Life of All the Living

1. Christ, the life of all the living,
   Christ, the death of death, our foe,
   Christ, yourself for me once giving

To the darkest depths of woe:
Through your suffering, death, and merit
Life eternal I inherit.
Thousand, thousand thanks are due,
Dearest Jesus, unto you.

2. You have suffered great affliction
   And have borne it patiently,
   Even death by crucifixion,
   Fully to atone for me;
   For you chose to be tormented
   That my doom should be prevented.
   Thousand, thousand thanks are due,
   Dearest Jesus, unto you.

3. Then, for all that bought my pardon,
   For the sorrows deep and sore,
   For the anguish in the garden,
   I will thank you evermore,
   Thank you for the groaning, sighing,
   For the bleeding and the dying,
   For that last triumphant cry,
   Praise you evermore on high.

Text: Kirchengesangbuch, Darmstadt

Hark! The Herald Angels Sing

1. Hark! The herald angels sing,
   "Glory to the newborn king;
   Peace on earth and mercy mild,
   God and sinners reconciled."
   Joyful, all you nations, rise;

Join the triumph of the skies;
With angelic hosts proclaim,
"Christ is born in Bethlehem!"
Hark! The herald angels sing,
"Glory to the newborn king!"

2. Christ, by highest heav'n adored,
   Christ, the everlasting Lord,
   Late in time behold him come,
   Offspring of a virgin's womb.
   Veiled in flesh the Godhead see!
   Hail, incarnate deity!
   Pleased as man with us to dwell,
   Jesus, our Emmanuel!
   Hark! The herald angels sing,
   "Glory to the newborn king!"

3. Hail the heav'n-born Prince of Peace!
   Hail the sun of righteousness!
   Light and life to all he brings,
   Ris'n with healing in his wings.
   Mild he lays his glory by,
   Born that we no more may die,
   Born to raise each child of earth,
   Born to give us second birth.
   Hark! The herald angels sing,
   "Glory to the newborn king!"

Text: Charles Wesley

Holy, Holy, Holy

1. Holy, holy, holy, Lord God Almighty!
   Early in the morning our song shall rise to
   thee.
   Holy, holy, holy, merciful and mighty!
   God in three Persons, blessed Trinity!

2. Holy, holy, holy! All the saints adore thee,
   Casting down their golden crowns around the
   glassy sea;
   Cherubim and seraphim falling down before
   thee,
   Which wert and art and evermore shalt be.

3. Holy, holy, holy! Though the darkness hide
   thee,
   Though the eye made blind by sin thy glory
   may not see,
   Only thou art holy; there is none beside thee,
   Perfect in pow'r, in love and purity.

4. Holy, holy, holy, Lord God Almighty!
   All thy works shall praise thy name in earth
   and sky and sea.
   Holy, holy, holy, merciful and mighty!
   God in three Persons, blessed Trinity!

Text: John B. Dykes

How Sweet the Name of Jesus Sounds

1. How sweet the name of Jesus sounds
   In a believer's ear!
   It soothes our sorrows, heals our wounds,
   And drives away all fear.

2. It makes the wounded spirit whole
   And calms the heart's unrest;
   It's manna to the hungry soul
   And to the weary, rest.

3. Dear name! The rock on which I build,
   My shield and hiding place;
   My never failing treasury filled
   With boundless stores of grace.

4. By you my prayers acceptance gain
   Although with sin defiled.
   The devil charges me in vain,
   And God calls me his child.

5. O Jesus, shepherd, guardian, friend,
   My Prophet, Priest, and King,
   My Lord, my life, my way, my end,
   Accept the praise I bring.

6. I praise in weakness from afar—
   How cold my warmest thought!
   But when I see you as you are,
   I'll praise you as I ought.

7. Till then I would your love proclaim
   With every fleeting breath;

And may the music of your name
Refresh my soul in death!

Text: Alexander R. Reinagle

Jesus Christ Is Risen Today

1. Jesus Christ is ris'n today, Alleluia!
   Our triumphant holy day, Alleluia!
   Who did once upon the cross, Alleluia!
   Suffer to redeem our loss. Alleluia!

2. Hymns of praise then let us sing, Alleluia!
   Unto Christ, our heav'nly king, Alleluia!
   Who endured the cross and grave, Alleluia!
   Sinners to redeem and save. Alleluia!

3. But the pains which he endured, Alleluia!
   Our salvation have procured; Alleluia!
   Now above the sky he's king, Alleluia!
   Where the angels ever sing. Alleluia!

4. Sing we to our God above, Alleluia!
   Praise eternal as his love; Alleluia!
   Praise him, all you heav'nly host, Alleluia!
   Father, Son, and Holy Ghost. Alleluia!

Text: Lyra Davidica

Joy to the World

1. Joy to the world, the Lord is come!
   Let earth receive its King;
   Let every heart prepare him room
   And heav'n and nature sing,
   And heav'n and nature sing,

And heav'n, and heav'n and nature sing.

2. Joy to the earth, the Savior reigns!
   Let all their songs employ
   While fields and floods, rocks, hills, and plains
   Repeat the sounding joy,
   Repeat the sounding joy,
   Repeat, repeat the sounding joy.

3. No more let sin and sorrow grow
   Nor thorns infest the ground:
   He comes to make his blessings flow
   Far as the curse is found,
   Far as the curse is found,
   Far as, far as the curse is found.

4. He rules the world with truth and grace
   And makes the nations prove
   The glories of his righteousness
   And wonders of his love,
   And wonders of his love,
   And wonders, wonders of his love.

Text: Isaac Watts

Just as I Am, without One Plea

1. Just as I am, without one plea
   But that thy blood was shed for me
   And that thou bidd'st me come to thee,
   O Lamb of God, I come, I come.

2. Just as I am and waiting not
   To rid my soul of one dark blot,
   To thee, whose blood can cleanse each spot,

O Lamb of God, I come, I come.

3. Just as I am, though tossed about
   With many a conflict, many a doubt,
   Fightings and fears within, without,
   O Lamb of God, I come, I come.

4. Just as I am, poor, wretched, blind;
   Sight, riches, healing of the mind,
   Yea, all I need, in thee to find,
   O Lamb of God, I come, I come.

5. Just as I am, thou wilt receive,
   Wilt welcome, pardon, cleanse, relieve;
   Because thy promise I believe,
   O Lamb of God, I come, I come.

6. Just as I am; thy love unknown
   Has broken ev'ry barrier down;
   Now to be thine, yea, thine alone,
   O Lamb of God, I come, I come.

Text: William B. Bradbury

Now Thank We All Our God

1. Now thank we all our God
   With hearts and hands and voices,
   Who wondrous things has done,
   In whom his world rejoices;
   Who from our mothers' arms
   Has blest us on our way
   With countless gifts of love
   And still is ours today.

2. Oh, may this bounteous God
   Through all our life be near us,
   With ever joyful hearts
   And blessed peace to cheer us
   And keep us in his grace
   And guide us when perplexed
   And free us from all harm
   In this world and the next!

3. All praise and thanks to God
   The Father now be given,
   The Son, and him who reigns
   With them is highest heaven,
   The one eternal God,
   Whom earth and heaven adore;
   For thus it was, is now,
   And shall be evermore.

Text: Johann Cruger

O God of God, O Light of Light

1. O God of God, O light of light,
   O Prince of Peace and King of kings:
   To you in heaven's glory bright
   The song of praise forever rings.
   To him who shares the Father's throne,
   The Lamb once slain but raised again,
   Be all the glory he has won,
   All thanks and praise! Amen, amen.

2. For deep in prophets' sacred page,
   And grand in poets' winged word,

Slowly in type, from age to age
The nations saw their coming Lord;
Till through the deep Judean night
Rang out the song, "Goodwill to men!"
Sung once by firstborn sons of light,
It echoes now, "Goodwill!" Amen.

3. That life of truth, those deeds of love,
That death so steeped in hate and scorn
These all are past, and now above
He reigns, our king first crowned with thorn.
Lift up your heads, O mighty gates!
So sang that host beyond our ken.
Lift up your heads, your king awaits.
We lift them up. Amen, amen.

4. Then raise to Christ a mighty song,
And shout his name, his glories tell!
Sing, heavenly host, your praise prolong,
And all on earth, your anthem swell!
All hail, O Lamb for sinners slain!
Forever let the song ascend!
All hail, O Lamb enthroned to reign
All hail, all hail! Amen, amen.

Text: John Julian

Oh, Come, All Ye Faithful

1. Oh, come, all ye faithful,
Joyful and triumphant!
Oh, come ye, oh, come ye to Bethlehem;
Come and behold him

Born the king of angels:
Oh, come, let us adore him,
Oh, come, let us adore him,
Oh, come, let us adore him,
Christ the Lord.

2. Highest, most holy,
Light of light eternal,
Born of a virgin,
A mortal he comes;
Son of the Father
Now in flesh appearing!
Oh, come, let us adore him,
Oh, come, let us adore him,
Oh, come, let us adore him,
Christ the Lord.

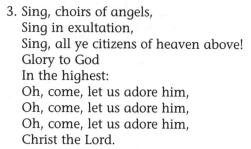

3. Sing, choirs of angels,
Sing in exultation,
Sing, all ye citizens of heaven above!
Glory to God
In the highest:
Oh, come, let us adore him,
Oh, come, let us adore him,
Oh, come, let us adore him,
Christ the Lord.

3. Yea, Lord, we greet thee,
Born this happy morning;
Jesus, to thee be glory giv'n!
Word of the Father,
Now in flesh appearing!

Oh, come, let us adore him,
Oh, come, let us adore him,
Oh, come, let us adore him,
Christ the Lord.

Text: John F. Wade

Oh, Come, Oh, Come, Emmanuel

1. Oh, come, oh, come, Emmanuel,
   And ransom captive Israel,
   That mourns in lonely exile here
   Until the Son of God appear.
   Rejoice! Rejoice! Emmanuel
   Shall come to you, O Israel!

2. Oh, come, our Wisdom from on high,
   Who ordered all things mightily;
   To us the path of knowledge show,
   And teach us in her ways to go.
   Rejoice! Rejoice! Emmanuel
   Shall come to you, O Israel!

3. Oh, come, oh, come, our Lord of might,
   Who to your tribes on Sinai's height
   In ancient times gave holy law,
   In cloud and majesty and awe.
   Rejoice! Rejoice! Emmanuel
   Shall come to you, O Israel!

4. Oh, come, O Rod of Jesse's stem,
   From ev'ry foe deliver them
   That trust your mighty pow'r to save;
   Bring them in vict'ry through the grave.

Rejoice! Rejoice! Emmanuel
Shall come to you, O Israel!

5. Oh, come, O Key of David, come,
   And open wide our heav'nly home;
   Make safe the way that leads on high,
   And close the path to misery.
   Rejoice! Rejoice! Emmanuel
   Shall come to you, O Israel!

6. Oh, come, our Dayspring from on high,
   And cheer us by your drawing nigh,
   Disperse the gloomy clouds of night,
   And death's dark shadows put to flight.
   Rejoice! Rejoice! Emmanuel
   Shall come to you, O Israel!

7. Oh, come, Desire of nations, bind
   In one the hearts of all mankind;
   Oh, bid our sad divisions cease,
   And be yourself our King of Peace.
   Rejoice! Rejoice! Emmanuel
   Shall come to you, O Israel!

Text: French Processional

Praise God, from Whom All Blessings Flow

Praise God, from whom all blessings flow;
Praise him, all creatures here below;
Praise him above, O heavenly host;
Praise Father, Son, and Holy Ghost.

Text: Louis Bourgeois

Rock of Ages, Cleft for Me

1. Rock of Ages, cleft for me,
   Let me hide myself in thee;
   Let the water and the blood,
   From thy riven side which flowed,
   Be of sin the double cure:
   Cleanse me from its guilt and power.

2. Not the labors of my hands
   Can fulfill thy law's demands;
   Could my zeal no respite know,
   Could my tears forever flow,
   All for sin could not atone;
   Thou must save, and thou alone.

3. Nothing in my hand I bring;
   Simply to thy cross I cling.
   Naked, come to thee for dress;
   Helpless, look to thee for grace;
   Foul, I to the fountain fly;
   Wash me, Savior, or I die.

4. While I draw this fleeting breath,
   When mine eyelids close in death,
   When I soar to worlds unknown,
   See thee on thy judgment throne,
   Rock of Ages, cleft for me,
   Let me hide myself in thee.

Text: Thomas Hastings

Silent Night

1. Silent night, holy night!
   All is calm, all is bright
   Round yon virgin mother and child.
   Holy Infant, so tender and mild,
   Sleep in heavenly peace,
   Sleep in heavenly peace.

2. Silent night, holy night!
   Shepherds quake at the sight;
   Glories stream from heaven afar,
   Heavenly hosts sing, Alleluia!
   Christ, the Savior, is born!
   Christ, the Savior, is born!

3. Silent night, holy night!
   Son of God, love's pure light
   Radiant beams from your holy face
   With the dawn of redeeming grace,
   Jesus, Lord, at your birth,
   Jesus, Lord, at your birth.

Text: Franz Gruber

Songs of Thankfulness and Praise

1. Songs of thankfulness and praise,
   Jesus, Lord, to thee we raise;
   Manifested by the star
   To the sages from afar,
   Branch of royal David's stem
   In thy birth at Bethlehem:
   Anthems be to thee addressed,

God in flesh made manifest.

2. Manifest at Jordan's stream,
   Prophet, Priest, and King supreme
   And at Cana wedding guest
   In thy Godhead manifest;
   Manifest in power divine,
   Changing water into wine;
   Anthems be to thee addressed
   God in flesh made manifest.

3. Manifest in making whole
   Palsied limbs and fainting soul;
   Manifest in valiant fight,
   Quelling all the devil's might;
   Manifest in gracious will,
   Ever bringing good from ill;
   Anthems be to thee addressed,
   God in flesh made manifest.

4. Grant us grace to see thee, Lord,
   Present in thy holy Word;
   Grace to imitate thee now
   And be pure, as pure art thou;
   That we might become like Thee
   At thy great epiphany
   And may praise thee, ever blest,
   God in flesh made manifest.

Text: Christopher Wordsworth

The Lord's My Shepherd, I'll Not Want

1. The Lord's my shepherd, I'll not want;

He makes me down to lie
In pastures green; He leadeth me
The quiet waters by.

2. My soul he doth restore again
   And me to walk doth make
   Within the paths of righteousness,
   Even for his own name's sake.

3. Yea, though I walk in death's dark vale,
   Yet will I fear no ill;
   For thou art with me, and thy rod
   And staff me comfort still.

4. My table thou hast furnished
   In presence of my foes;
   My head thou dost with oil anoint,
   And my cup overflows.

5. Goodness and mercy all my life
   Shall surely follow me;
   And in God's house forevermore
   My dwelling place shall be.

Text: William Gardiner

We All Believe in One True God, Father

1. We all believe in one true God,
   Father, Son, and Holy Ghost,
   Ever-present help in need,
   Praised by all the heavenly host;
   All he made his love enfolds,
   All creation he upholds.

2. We all believe in Jesus Christ,
   Son of God and Mary's son,
   Who descended from his throne
   And for us salvation won;
   By whose cross and death are we
   Rescued from all misery.

3. We all confess the Holy Ghost,
   Who from both in truth proceeds,
   Who sustains and comforts us
   In all trials, fears, and needs.
   Blest and holy Trinity,
   Praise forever yours shall be.

Text: Kirchengesangbuch

You Are the Way; to You Alone

1. You are the way; to you alone
   From sin and death we flee;
   And he who would the Father seek
   Your follower must be.

2. You are the truth; your Word alone
   True wisdom can impart;
   You only can inform the mind
   And purify the heart.

3. You are the life; the rending tomb
   Proclaims your conqu'ring arm;
   And those who put their trust in you
   Not death nor hell shall harm.

4. You are the way, the truth, the life;

Grant us that way to know,
That truth to keep, that life to win,
Whose joys eternal flow.

Text: George W. Doane

The Benedictus (Zechariah's Song)

Blessed be the Lord God of Israel; for He has visited and redeemed His people and has raised up a horn of salvation for us in the house of His servant David, as He spoke by the mouth of His holy prophets, who have been since the world began. That we should be saved from our enemies and from the hand of all who hate us; to perform the mercy promised to our fathers and remember His holy covenant, the oath that He swore to our father Abraham, to grant us that we, being delivered from the hand of our enemies, might serve Him without fear, in holiness and righteousness before Him all the days of our life.

[During Advent:] And You, child, will be called the prophet of the Most High; for You will go before the Lord to prepare His ways, to give knowledge of salvation to His people in the forgiveness of their sins, through the tender mercy of our God; when the day shall dawn upon us from on high to give light to them who sit in darkness and in the shadow of death, to guide our feet in the way of peace.

🌿 Nunc dimittis (Simeon's Song)

Lord, now let Your servant depart in peace according to Your word, for my eyes have seen Your salvation, which You have prepared before the face of all people, a Light to lighten the Gentiles, and the glory of Your people Israel.

Glory be to the Father and to the Son and to the Holy Ghost; as it was in the beginning, is now and ever shall be, world without end. Amen.

🌿 Te Deum laudamus

We praise You, O God; we acknowledge You to be the Lord; all the earth now worships You, the Father everlasting. To You all angels cry aloud, the heavens and all the powers therein.

To You cherubim and seraphim continually do cry: Holy, holy, holy, Lord God of Sabaoth; heaven and earth are full of the majesty of Your glory. The glorious company of the apostles praise You; the goodly fellowship of the prophets praise You. The noble army of martyrs praise You. The holy Church throughout all the world does acknowledge You: The Father of an infinite majesty; Your adorable true and only Son, also the Holy Ghost, the comforter. You are the King of glory, O Christ; You are the everlasting Son of the Father.

When You took upon Yourself to deliver man, You humbled Yourself to be born of a virgin. When You had overcome the sharpness of death, You opened the kingdom of heaven to all believers. You sit at the right hand of God in the glory of the Father. We believe that You will come to be our judge.

We therefore pray You to help Your servants, whom You have redeemed with Your precious blood. Make them to be numbered with Your saints in glory everlasting.

O Lord, save Your people and bless Your heritage. Govern them up forever. Day by day we magnify You. And we worship Your name ever, world without end. Vouchsafe, O Lord, to keep us this day without sin. O Lord, have mercy upon us, have mercy upon us. O Lord, let Your mercy be upon us, as our trust is in You. O Lord, in You have I trusted; let me never be confounded.

The Magnificat (Mary's Song)

My soul magnifies the Lord, and my spirit rejoices in God, my Savior; for He has regarded the lowliness of His handmaiden. For, behold, from this day all generations will call me blessed. For the Mighty One has done great things to me, and Holy is His name; and His mercy is on those who fear Him from generation to generation. He has shown strength with His arm; He has scattered the proud in the imagination of their hearts. He has cast down the mighty from their thrones, and has exalted the lowly. He has filled the hungry with good things, and the rich He has sent away empty. He has helped His servant Israel in remembrance of His mercy, as He spoke to our fathers, to Abraham, and to his seed forever.

Themes in the Selected Psalms

Christmas—98

Close of Day—4

Confession—51

Consolation and Comfort—38:9, 21–22;
    51:10–12; 102:1–2; 130:1–5

Easter—118:19–29

Evening—6

Forgiveness and Redemption—40:1–3; 32:1–5

Future—90

Mealtime, Asking a Blessing—145:15–16

Mealtime, Returning Thanks—136:1, 25;
    147:9–11

Morning—5

Peace and Hope—23, 16:11

Praise—30, 138

Righteousness—1

Morning Prayer

Sundays and Festivals: 1, 2, 8, 19, 27, 45,
62, 67, 72, 84, 98
Other Days: 18, 22, 24, 25, 28, 32, 50, 65, 73,
90, 92, 96, 100, 107, 119, 147, 148

Evening Prayer

Sundays and Festivals: 23, 110, 111, 114
Other Days: 38, 46, 51, 105, 116, 117, 118, 126,
130, 135, 136, 138, 139, 141, 143, 146

Close of the Day

Sundays and Festivals: 91, 133, 134
Other Days: 12, 16, 34, 77, 103

Affliction: 34, 130

Assurance of Forgiveness:
1, 103, 119:7–14, 119:
33-40

Comfort: 23, 90, 116,
118, 130

Confession: 30, 51, 102

Confidence and Trust:
16, 23, 25, 27, 37, 46,
62, 91, 121, 139

Encouragement: 73

Eternal Life: 16, 17, 23,
49, 116

Marriage: 45, 127

Mercy: 6, 25, 32, 36, 38,
73, 77, 102, 130, 143

Praise: 9, 18, 32, 40, 66,
92, 100, 116, 145

Prayer: 17, 86, 90 102, 142

Thanksgiving: 30, 31,
100, 116, 124, 126, 136

Trust: 23, 27, 62, 63, 71, 131

Salvation: 67, 128

Strength in the Face of
Tribulation: 3, 5, 10, 43,
54, 57

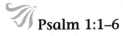

Psalm 1:1–6

(Righteousness)

Blessed is the man
who walks not in the counsel of the wicked,
    nor stands in the way of sinners
    nor sits in the seat of scoffers;
[2] but his delight is in the law of the LORD,
    and on His law he meditates day and night.
[3] He is like a tree
    planted by streams of water
that yields its fruit in its season,
    and its leaf does not wither.
In all that he does, he prospers.
[4] The wicked are not so,
    but are like chaff that the wind drives away.
[5] Therefore the wicked will not stand in the judgment,
    nor sinners in the congregation of the righteous;
[6] for the LORD knows the way of the righteous,
    but the way of the wicked will perish.

Psalm 4

(Close of the Day)

Answer me when I call, O God of my righteousness!
    You have given me relief when I was in distress.
    Be gracious to me and hear my prayer!
[2] O men, how long shall my honor be turned into
    shame?

55

How long will you love vain words and seek
    after lies? *Selah*

³But know that the Lord has set apart the godly for
    Himself;
    the Lord hears when I call to Him.

⁴Be angry, and do not sin;
    ponder in your own hearts on your beds,
        and be silent. *Selah*

⁵Offer right sacrifices,
    and put your trust in the Lord.

⁶There are many who say, "Who will show us
        some good?
    Lift up the light of Your face upon us, O Lord!"

⁷You have put more joy in my heart
    than they have when their grain and wine
abound.

⁸In peace I will both lie down and sleep;
    for You alone, O Lord, make me dwell in safety.

Psalm 5

(Morning)

Give ear to my words, O Lord;
    consider my groaning.

²Give attention to the sound of my cry,
    my King and my God,
    for to You do I pray.

³O Lord, in the morning You hear my voice;
    in the morning I prepare a sacrifice for You
        and watch.

⁴For You are not a God who delights in wickedness;
    evil may not dwell with You.

⁵The boastful shall not stand before Your eyes;
    You hate all evildoers.

⁶You destroy those who speak lies;
    the LORD abhors the bloodthirsty and deceitful man.

⁷But I, through the abundance of Your steadfast love,
    will enter Your house.

I will bow down toward Your holy temple
    in the fear of You.

⁸Lead me, O LORD, in Your righteousness
    because of my enemies;
    make Your way straight before me.

⁹For there is no truth in their mouth;
    their inmost self is destruction;

their throat is an open grave;
    they flatter with their tongue.

¹⁰Make them bear their guilt, O God;
    let them fall by their own counsels;

because of the abundance of their transgressions
    cast them out,
    for they have rebelled against You.

¹¹But let all who take refuge in You rejoice;
    let them ever sing for joy,

and spread Your protection over them,
    that those who love
    Your name may exult in You.

¹²For You bless the righteous, O Lord;
    You cover him with favor as with a shield.

Psalm 6

(Evening)

O LORD, rebuke me not in Your anger,
    nor discipline me in Your wrath.

²Be gracious to me, O LORD, for I am languishing;
    heal me, O LORD, for my bones are troubled.

³My soul also is greatly troubled.
    But You, O LORD—how long?

⁴Turn, O LORD, deliver my life;
    save me for the sake of Your steadfast love.

⁵For in death there is no remembrance of You;
    in Sheol who will give You praise?

⁶I am weary with my moaning;
    every night I flood my bed with tears;
    I drench my couch with my weeping.

⁷My eye wastes away because of grief;
    it grows weak because of all my foes.

⁸Depart from me, all you workers of evil,
    for the LORD has heard the sound of my weeping.

⁹The Lord has heard my plea;
    the Lord accepts my prayer.

¹⁰All my enemies shall be ashamed and greatly
    troubled;
    they shall turn back and be put to shame in a
    moment.

 **Psalm 23**

(Peace and Hope)

The LORD is my shepherd; I shall not want.
² He makes me lie down in green pastures.

He leads me beside still waters.
³ He restores my soul.

He leads me in paths of righteousness
for His name's sake.

⁴ Even though I walk through the valley of
the shadow of death,
I will fear no evil,

for You are with me;
Your rod and Your staff,
they comfort me.

⁵ You prepare a table before me
in the presence of my enemies;

You anoint my head with oil;
my cup overflows.

⁶ Surely goodness and mercy shall follow me
all the days of my life,

and I shall dwell in the house of the LORD
forever.

Psalm 30

(Praise)

I will extol you, O Lord, for You have drawn me up
   and have not let my foes rejoice over me.
2 O Lord my God, I cried to You for help,
   and You have healed me.
3 O Lord, You have brought up my soul
     from Sheol;
   You restored me to life from among those
     who go down to the pit.
4 Sing praises to the Lord, O you His saints,
     and give thanks to His holy name.
5 For His anger is but for a moment,
   and His favor is for a life time.
Weeping may tarry for the night,
   but joy comes with the morning.
6 As for me, I said in my prosperity,
   "I shall never be moved."
7 By Your favor, O Lord,
     You made my mountain stand strong;
You hid your face;
   I was dismayed.
8 To you, O Lord, I cry,
   and to the Lord I plead for mercy:
9 "What profit is there in my death,
     if I go down to the pit?
Will the dust praise You?
   Will it tell of your faithfulness?
10 Hear, O Lord, and be merciful to me!

O LORD, be my helper!"

¹¹You have turned for me my mourning into dancing;
  You have loosed my sackcloth
  and clothed me with gladness,
¹²that my glory may sing Your praise and not be silent.
  O LORD my God, I will give thanks to You forever!

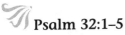 **Psalm 32:1–5**

(Forgiveness and Redemption)

Blessed is the one whose transgression is forgiven,
  whose sin is covered.
²Blessed is the man against whom the LORD counts no
  iniquity,
  and in whose spirit there is no deceit.
³For when I kept silent, my bones wasted away
  through my groaning all day long.
⁴For day and night Your hand was heavy upon me;
  my stregnth was dried up as by the heat of
  summer. *Selah*
⁵I acknowledged my sin to You,
  and I did not cover my iniquity;
I said, "I will confess my transgressions to the LORD,"
  and You forgave the iniquity of my sin.

Psalm 38:9, 21–22

(Consolation and Comfort)

⁹O Lord, all my longing is before You;
  my sighing is not hidden from You.

²¹Do not forsake me, O LORD!
  O my God, be not far from me!
²²Make haste to help me,
  O Lord, my salvation!

Psalm 40:1–3

(Forgiveness and Redemption)

I waited patiently for the LORD;
  He inclined to me and heard my cry.
²He drew me up from the pit of destruction,
  out of the miry bog,
and set my feet upon a rock,
  making my steps secure.
³He put a new song in my mouth,
  a song of praise to our God.
Many will see and fear,
  and put their trust in the LORD.

Psalm 51

(Confession)

Have mercy on me, O God,
    according to Your steadfast love;
according to Your abundant mercy
    blot out my transgressions.

²Wash me thoroughly from my iniquity,
    and cleanse me from my sin!

³For I know my transgressions,
    and my sin is ever before me.

⁴Against You, You only, have I sinned
    and done what is evil in Your sight,

so that You may be justified in Your words
    and blameless in Your judgment.

⁵Behold, I was brought forth in iniquity,
    and in sin did my mother conceive me.

⁶Behold, You delight in truth in the inward being,
    and You teach me wisdom in the secret heart.

⁷Purge me with hyssop, and I shall be clean;
    wash me, and I shall be whiter than snow.

⁸Let me hear joy and gladness;
    let the bones that You have broken rejoice.

⁹Hide your face from my sins,
    and blot out all my iniquities.

¹⁰Create in me a clean heart, O God,
    and renew a right spirit within me.

¹¹Cast me not away from Your presence,
    and take not Your Holy Spirit from me.

¹²Restore to me the joy of Your salvation,
   and uphold me with a willing spirit.
¹³Then I will teach transgressors Your ways,
   and sinners will return to You.
¹⁴Deliver me from bloodguiltiness, O God,
      O God of my salvation,
   and my tongue will sing aloud of your
      righteousness.
¹⁵O Lord, open my lips,
   and my mouth will declare your praise.
¹⁶For you will not delight in sacrifice, or I would give it;
   you will not be pleased with a burnt offering.
¹⁷The sacrifices of God are a broken spirit;
   a broken and contrite heart, O God, you will not
      despise.
¹⁸Do good to Zion in your good pleasure;
   build up the walls of Jerusalem;
¹⁹then will you delight in right sacrifices,
   in burnt offerings and whole burnt offerings;
   then bulls will be offered on your altar.

 Psalm 90

   (Future)

Lord, You have been our dwelling place
   in all generations.
²Before the mountains were brought forth,
   or ever You had formed the earth and the world,
   from everlasting to everlasting You are God.
³You return man to dust

and say, "Return, O children of man!"

⁴For a thousand years in Your sight
   are but as yesterday when it is past,
   or as a watch in the night.

⁵You sweep them away as with a flood; they are
      like a dream,
   like grass that is renewed in the morning:

⁶in the morning it flourishes and is renewed;
   in the evening it fades and withers.

⁷For we are brought to an end by Your anger;
   by Your wrath we are dismayed.

⁸You have set our iniquities before You,
   our secret sins in the light of Your presence.

⁹For all our days pass away under Your wrath;
   we bring our years to an end like a sigh.

¹⁰The years of our life are seventy,
   or even by reason of strength eighty;
   yet their span is but toil and trouble;
   they are soon gone, and we fly away.

¹¹Who considers the power of Your anger,
   and Your wrath according to the fear of You?

¹²So teach us to number our days
   that we may get a heart of wisdom.

¹³Return, O LORD! How long?
   Have pity on Your servants!

¹⁴Satisfy us in the morning with Your steadfast love,
   that we may rejoice and be glad all our days.

¹⁵Make us glad for as many days as You have
      afflicted us,
   and for as many years as we have seen evil.

¹⁶Let Your work be shown to Your servants,

and Your glorious power to their children.

¹⁷Let the favor of the Lord our God be upon us,
and establish the work of our hands upon us;
yes, establish the work of our hands!

 **Psalm 98**

(Christmas)

Oh sing to the LORD a new song,
for He has done marvelous things!
His right hand and His holy arm
have worked salvation for Him.

²The LORD has made known His salvation;
He has revealed His righteousness in the sight of
the nations.

³He has remembered His steadfast love and faithful
ness to the house of Israel.
All the ends of the earth have seen
the salvation of our God.

⁴Make a joyful noise to the LORD, all the earth;
break forth into joyous song and sing praises!

⁵Sing praises to the LORD with the lyre,
with the lyre and the sound of melody!

⁶With trumpets and the sound of the horn
make a joyful noise before the King, the LORD!

⁷Let the sea roar, and all that fills it;
the world and those who dwell in it!

⁸Let the rivers clap their hands;
let the hills sing for joy together

⁹before the LORD, for He comes

to judge the earth.
He will judge the world with righteousness,
and the peoples with equity.

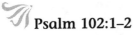

Psalm 102:1–2
(Consolation and Comfort)

Hear my prayer, O LORD;
let my cry come to You!

²Do not hide your face from me
in the day of my distress!
Incline Your ear to me;
answer me speedily in the day when I call!

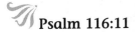

Psalm 116:11

(Peace and Hope)

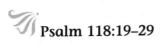

You make known to me the path of life;
in Your presence there is fullness of joy;
at Your right hand are pleasures fovevermore.

Psalm 118:19–29
(Easter)

Open to me the gates of righteousness,
that I may enter through them
and give thanks to the LORD.

²⁰This is the gate of the L<small>ORD</small>;
   the righteous shall enter through it.
²¹I thank You that You have answered me
   and have become my salvation.
²²The stone that the builders rejected
   has become the cornerstone.
²³This is the L<small>ORD</small>'s doing;
   it is marvelous in our eyes.
²⁴This is the day that the L<small>ORD</small> has made;
   let us rejoice and be glad in it.
²⁵Save us, we pray, O L<small>ORD</small>!
   O L<small>ORD</small>, we pray, give us success!
²⁶Blessed is He who comes in the name of the L<small>ORD</small>!
   We bless You from the house of the L<small>ORD</small>.
²⁷The L<small>ORD</small> is God,
   and He has made His light to shine upon us.
Bind the festal sacrifice with cords,
   up to the horns of the altar!
²⁸You are my God, and I will give thanks to You;
   you are my God; I will extol You.
²⁹Oh give thanks to the L<small>ORD</small>, for He is good;
   for His steadfast love endures forever!

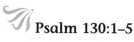

Psalm 130:1–5

(Consolation and Comfort)

Out of the depths I cry to You, O L<small>ORD</small>!
   ²O Lord, hear my voice!
Let Your ears be attentive
   to the voice of my pleas for mercy!

³If You, O LORD, should mark iniquities,
O Lord, who could stand?
⁴But with You there is forgiveness,
that You may be feared.
⁵I wait for the LORD, my soul waits,
and in His word I hope.

 ## Psalm 136:1, 25; 147:9–11

(Meal-Returning Thanks)

¹Give thanks to the LORD, for He is good,
for His steadfast love endures forever.

²⁵He who gives food to all flesh,
for His steadfast love endures forever.

^{147:9}He gives to the beasts their food,
and to the young ravens that cry.
¹⁰His delight is not in the strength of the horse,
nor His pleasure in the legs of a man,
¹¹but the LORD takes pleasure in those who fear Him,
in those who hope in His steadfast love.

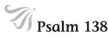 ## Psalm 138

(Praise)

I give You thanks, O LORD, with my whole heart;
before the gods I sing Your praise;
²I bow down toward Your holy temple

and give thanks to Your name for Your steadfast
   love and your faithfulness,
for You have exalted above all things
   Your name and Your word.
[3]On the day I called, You answered me;
   my strength of soul You increased.
[4]All the kings of the earth shall give You thanks,
     O LORD,
   for they have heard the words of Your mouth,
[5]and they shall sing of the ways of the LORD,
   for great is the glory of the LORD.
[6]For though the LORD is high, He regards the lowly,
   but the haughty He knows from afar.
[7]Though I walk in the midst of trouble,
   You preserve my life;
You stretch out Your hand against the wrath of my
     enemies,
   and Your right hand delivers me.
[8]The LORD will fulfill His purpose for me;
   Your steadfast love, O LORD, endures forever.
   Do not forsake the work of Your hands.

Psalm 145:15–16

(Meal–Asking a Blessing)
The eyes of all look to You,
   and You give them their food in due season.
[16]You open Your hand;
   You satisfy the desire of every living thing.

The Selection of Scripture Lessons are arranged according to their order in the Bible.

The following are suggested for themes in Christian life and in the church year:

The Birth of Jesus:
   Luke 2:1–20
**The Death and Burial
   of Jesus:**
   John 19:16–42
The Resurrection of Jesus:
   Luke 24:1–8
Assurance:
   Job 19:21–27;
   Romans 8:31–39;
   Psalm 103:8–12
Beatitudes:
   Matthew 5:3–11
Children:
   Deuteronomy 6:4–7;
   Matthew 18:2–6
Christian Life:
   Ephesians 5:1–4;
   Jude 20–25
Consolation:
   Isaiah 43:1–3;
   Psalm 103:8–12;
   Hebrews 12:1–4

Encouragement:
   Ephesians 6:10–17;
   Hebrews 10:35–36;
   Hebrews 12:1–11;
   1 Peter 1:3–9
Friendship:
   Ecclesiastes 4:9–11;
   Ephesians 4:29–32
Future:
   Matthew 6:31–34;
   Psalm 139:1–6
Grief/Loss:
   2 Samuel 22:2–4;
   1 Corinthians 15:51–57;
   1 Thessalonians 4:13–18
Loneliness:
   Deuteronomy 31:8;
   Matthew 28:20
Love:
   John 3:16;
   1 Corinthians 13;
   Ephesians 2:4–5;
   Ephesians 5:2;

1 John 4:7–10

Marriage:
Matthew 19:4–6;
Ephesians 5:22–33

Money:
1 Timothy 6:6–10

Peace and Hope:
Proverbs 3:5–8;
1 John 3:1–2

Prayer:
Mark 11:24–26

Protection:
John 17:11–15

Repentance and Forgiveness:
Psalm 32:1–5;
Romans 5:1–8; (see
also 1 Timothy 1:15)

Salvation:
John 3:13–21;
John 14:1–6;
Romans 1:16–17;
Ephesians 2:8–9;
1 John 4:9–10

Self-Esteem:
Isaiah 43:1–3;

Sick and Infirm:
Lamentations 3:22–26

Sin and Temptation:
1 Corinthians 10:13;
1 John 1:6–9

Single:
Psalm 62:5–8

Stress:
Psalm 131;
Philippians 4:5–7

Trust:
Psalm 37:3–4

Widow:
1 Timothy 5:5

Witnessing:
Luke 21:13–15;
Romans 1:16–17

Work:
Colossians 3:23, 24

Morning Prayer

Then Moses and the people of Israel sang this
    song to the LORD, saying,
"I will sing to the LORD, for He has triumphed
    gloriously;
the horse and his rider He has thrown into
    the sea.
The LORD is my strength and my song,
    and He has become my salvation;
this is my God, and I will praise Him,
my father's God, and I will exalt Him.
The LORD is a man of war;
the LORD is His name.
"Pharaoh's chariots and his host He cast
    into the sea,
and his chosen officers were sunk in the
    Red Sea.
The floods covered them;
they went down into the depths like a stone.
Your right hand, O LORD, glorious in power,
Your right hand, O LORD, shatters the enemy
In the greatness of Your majesty You overthrow
    Your adversaries;
You send out Your fury; it consumes them
    like stubble.
At the blast of Your nostrils the waters

piled up;

the floods stood up in a heap;

the deeps congealed in the heart of the sea.

The enemy said, 'I will pursue, I will overtake,

I will divide the spoil, my desire shall have its
fill of them.

I will draw my sword; my hand shall destroy
them.'

You blew with Your wind; the sea covered them;

they sank like lead in the mighty waters.

"Who is like You, O Lord, among the gods?

Who is like You, majestic in holiness,

awesome in glorious deeds, doing wonders?"

Exodus 15:1–11

Early Evening Prayer

And the LORD said to Moses, "I have heard the grumbling of the people of Israel. Say to them, 'At twilight you shall eat meat, and in the morning you shall be filled with bread. Then you shall know that I am the LORD your God.'"

In the evening quail came up and covered the camp, and in the morning dew lay around the camp. And when the dew had gone up, there was on the face of the wilderness a fine, flake-like thing, fine as frost on the ground. When the people of Israel saw it, they said to one another, "What is it?" For they did not know what it was. And Moses said to them, "It is the bread that the LORD has given you to eat. This is what the LORD has commanded: 'Gather of it, each one of you, as much as he can eat. You shall each take an omer, according to the number of the persons that each of you has in his tent.'" And the people of Israel did so. They gathered, some more, some less. But when they measured it with an omer, whoever gathered much had nothing left over, and whoever gathered little had no lack. Each of them gathered as much as he could eat. And Moses said to them, "Let no one leave any of it over till the morning." But they did not listen to Moses. Some left part of it till the morning, and it bred worms and stank. And Moses was angry with them. Morning by morning they gathered it, each as much as he could eat; but when the sun grew hot, it melted. Now the house of Israel called its name manna. It was like coriander seed, white, and the taste of it was like wafers made with honey.

Exodus 16:11–21, 31

Children

Hear, O Israel: The LORD our God, the LORD is one. You shall love the LORD your God with all your heart and with all your soul and with all your might. And these words that I command you today shall be on your heart. You shall teach them diligently to your children, and shall talk of them when you sit in your house, and when you walk by the way, and when you lie down, and when you rise.

Deuteronomy 6:4–7

Loneliness

It is the LORD who goes before you. He will be with you; He will not leave you or forsake you. Do not fear or be dismayed.

Deuteronomy 31:8

Grief

The LORD is my rock and my fortress and my
deliverer, my God, my rock, in whom I take
   refuge,
my shield, and the horn of my salvation,
my stronghold and my refuge,
my savior; You save me from violence.
I call upon the LORD, who is worthy to be
   praised,
and I am saved from my enemies.

                        2 Samuel 22:2–4

 **Assurance**

Have mercy on me, have mercy on me,
   O you my friends,
for the hand of God has touched me!
Why do you, like God, pursue me?
   Why are you not satisfied with my flesh?
"Oh that my words were written!
   Oh that they were inscribed in a book!
Oh that with an iron pen and lead
   they were engraved in the rock forever!
For I know that my Redeemer lives,

and at the last He will stand upon the earth.
And after my skin has been thus destroyed,
    yet in my flesh I shall see God,
whom I shall see for myself,
    and my eyes shall behold, and not another.
    My heart faints within me!"

Job 19:21–27

 Repentance

Blessed is the one whose transgression is forgiven,
    whose sin is covered.
Blessed is the man against whom the LORD
        counts no iniquity,
    and in whose spirit there is no deceit.
For when I kept silent, my bones wasted away
    through my groaning all day long.
For day and night Your hand was heavy upon
    me; my strength was dried up as by the heat of
        summer.
I acknowledged my sin to You,
    and I did not cover my iniquity;
I said, "I will confess my transgressions to the
    LORD,"
    and You forgave the iniquity of my sin.

Psalm 32:1–5

Trust

Trust in the Lord, and do good;
> dwell in the land and befriend faithfulness.

Delight yourself in the Lord,
> and He will give you the desires of your
> > heart.

Psalm 37:3–4

 Single

For God alone, O my soul, wait in silence,
> for my hope is from Him.

He only is my rock and my salvation,
> my fortress; I shall not be shaken.

On God rests my salvation and my glory;
> my mighty rock, my refuge is God.

Trust in Him at all times, O people;
> pour out your heart before Him;
> God is a refuge for us.

Psalm 62:5–8

 Consolation

The Lord is merciful and gracious,
> slow to anger and abounding in steadfast

love.

He will not always chide,
    nor will He keep His anger forever.

He does not deal with us according to our sins,
    nor repay us according to our iniquities.

For as high as the heavens are above the earth,
    so great is His steadfast love toward those
    who fear Him;

as far as the east is from the west,
    so far does He remove our transgressions
    from us.

Psalm 103:8–12

 Stress

O Lord, my heart is not lifted up;
    my eyes are not raised too high;
I do not occupy myself with things
    too great and too marvelous for me.

But I have calmed and quieted my soul,
    like a weaned child with its mother;
    like a weaned child is my soul within me.

O Israel, hope in the Lord
    from this time forth and forevermore.

Psalm 131

Future

O Lord, You have searched me and known me!
You know when I sit down and when I rise up;
    You discern my thoughts from afar.
You search out my path and my lying down
    And are acquainted with all my ways.
Even before a word is on my tongue,
    behold, O Lord, You know it altogether.
You hem me in, behind and before,
    and lay Your hand upon me.
Such knowledge is too wonderful for me;
    It is high; I cannot attain it.

Psalm 139:1–6

 Peace

Trust in the Lord with all your heart,
    and do not lean on your own understanding.
In all your ways acknowledge Him,
    and He will make straight your paths.
Be not wise in your own eyes;
    fear the Lord, and turn away from evil.
It will be healing to your flesh
    and refreshment to your bones.

Proverbs 3:5–8

Friendship

Two are better than one, because they have a good reward for their toil. For if they fall, one will lift up his fellow. But woe to him who is alone when he falls and has not another to lift him up! Again, if two lie together, they keep warm, but how can one keep warm alone?

Ecclesiastes 4:9–11

Morning Prayer

You will say in that day:
"I will give thanks to You, O Lord,
    for though You were angry with me,
Your anger turned away,
    that You might comfort me.
"Behold, God is my salvation;
    I will trust, and will not be afraid;
for the Lord God is my strength and my song,
    and He has become my salvation."

With joy you will draw water from the wells of salvation. And you will say in that day:
"Give thanks to the Lord,
    call upon His name,
make known His deeds among the peoples,
    proclaim that His name is exalted.
"Sing praises to the Lord, for He has done
      gloriously;

let this be made known in all the earth.
Shout, and sing for joy, O inhabitant of Zion,
    for great in your midst is the Holy One of
        Israel."

Isaiah 12:1–6

Early Evening

On this mountain the LORD of hosts will make
    for all peoples
a feast of rich food, a feast of well-aged wine,
of rich food full of marrow, of aged wine well
    refined.
    And He will swallow up on this mountain
the covering that is cast over all peoples,
the veil that is spread over all nations.
    He will swallow up death forever;
and the LORD God will wipe away tears from all
    faces,
and the reproach of His people He will take
    away from all the earth,
for the LORD has spoken.
    It will be said on that day,
"Behold, this is our God; we have waited for
    Him, that He might save us.
This is the LORD; we have waited for Him;
let us be glad and rejoice in His salvation.

Isaiah 25:6–9

 **Self-Esteem**

But now thus says the LORD,
    He who created you, O Jacob,
    He who formed you, O Israel:
"Fear not, for I have redeemed you;
    I have called you by name, you are mine.
When you pass through the waters, I will be
        with you;
    and through the rivers, they shall not over-
        whelm you;
when you walk through fire you shall not be
        burned,
    and the flame shall not consume you.
For I am the LORD your God,
    the Holy One of Israel, your Savior.

                             Isaiah 43:1–3

 Sick

    The steadfast love of the LORD never ceases;
His mercies never come to an end;
    they are new every morning;
great is Your faithfulness.
    "The LORD is my portion," says my soul,
"therefore I will hope in Him."

The LORD is good to those who wait for Him,
to the soul who seeks Him.

It is good that one should wait quietly
for the salvation of the LORD.

Lamentations 3:22–26

 Close of the Day

Who is a God like You, pardoning iniquity
and passing over transgression
for the remnant of His inheritance?

He does not retain His anger forever,
because He delights in steadfast love.

He will again have compassion on us;
He will tread our iniquities under foot.

You will cast all our sins
into the depths of the sea.

You will show faithfulness to Jacob
and steadfast love to Abraham,

as You have sworn to our fathers
from the days of old.

Micah 7:18–20

 Beatitudes

"Blessed are the poor in spirit, for theirs is the
kingdom of heaven.

"Blessed are those who mourn, for they shall be comforted.

"Blessed are the meek, for they shall inherit the earth.

"Blessed are those who hunger and thirst for righteousness, for they shall be satisfied.

"Blessed are the merciful, for they shall receive mercy.

"Blessed are the pure in heart, for they shall see God.

"Blessed are the peacemakers, for they shall be called sons of God.

"Blessed are those who are persecuted for righteousness' sake, for theirs is the kingdom of heaven.

"Blessed are you when others revile you and persecute you and utter all kinds of evil against you falsely on my account."

Matthew 5:3–11

 Noon Prayer

[Jesus spoke to them saying,] "You are the salt of the earth, but if salt has lost its taste, how shall its saltiness be restored? It is no longer good for anything except to be thrown out and trampled under people's feet.

"You are the light of the world. A city set on a

hill cannot be hidden. Nor do people light a lamp and put it under a basket, but on a stand, and it gives light to all in the house. In the same way, let your light shine before others, so that they may see your good works and give glory to your Father who is in heaven."

Matthew 5:13–16

 Future

[Jesus said,] "Therefore do not be anxious, saying, 'What shall we eat?' or 'What shall we drink?' or 'What shall we wear?' For the Gentiles seek after all these things, and your heavenly Father knows that you need them all. But seek first the kingdom of God and His righteousness, and all these things will be added to you.

"Therefore do not be anxious about tomorrow, for tomorrow will be anxious for itself. Sufficient for the day is its own trouble."

Matthew 6:31–34

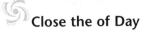
Close the of Day

[Jesus said,] "Come to Me, all who labor and are heavy laden, and I will give you rest. Take My yoke upon you, and learn from Me, for I am gentle and lowly in heart, and you will find rest for your souls. For My yoke is easy, and My burden is light."

Matthew 11:28–30

Noon Prayer

That same day Jesus went out of the house and sat beside the sea. And great crowds gathered about Him, so that He got into a boat and sat down. And the whole crowd stood on the beach. And He told them many things in parables, saying: "A sower went out to sow. And as he sowed, some seeds fell along the path, and the birds came and devoured them. Other seeds fell on rocky ground, where they did not have much soil, and immediately they sprang up, since they had no depth of soil, but when the sun rose they were scorched. And since they had no root, they withered away. Other seeds fell among thorns, and the thorns grew up and choked them. Other seeds fell on good soil and produced grain, some a hundredfold, some sixty, some thirty. He who has ears, let him hear.

"Hear then the parable of the sower: When anyone hears the word of the kingdom and does not understand it, the evil one comes and snatches away what has been sown in his heart. This is what was sown along the path. As for what was sown on rocky ground, this is the one who hears the word and immediately receives it with joy, yet he has no root in himself, but endures for a while, and when tribulation or persecution arises on account of the word, immediately he falls away. As for what was sown among thorns, this is the one who hears the word, but the cares of the world and the deceitfulness of riches choke the word, and it proves unfruitful. As for what was sown on good soil, this is the one who hears the word and understands it. He indeed bears fruit and yields, in one case a hundredfold, in another sixty, and in another thirty.

Matthew 13:1–9, 18–23

 Early Evening

Now when it was evening, the disciples came to [Jesus] and said, "This is a desolate place, and the day is now over; send the crowds away to go into the villages and buy food for themselves." But Jesus said, "They need not go away; you give them something to eat." They said to Him, "We have only five loaves here and two fish." And He said, "Bring them here to Me." Then He ordered the crowds to sit down on the grass, and taking the five loaves and the two fish, He looked up to heaven and said a blessing. Then He broke the loaves and gave them to the disciples, and the disciples gave them to the crowds. And they all ate and were satisfied. And they took up twelve baskets full of the broken pieces left over. And those who ate were about five thousand men, besides women and children.

Matthew 14:15–21

Children

And calling to Him a child, [Jesus] put him in the midst of them and said, "Truly, I say to you, unless you turn and become like children, you will never enter the kingdom of heaven. Whoever humbles himself like this child is the greatest in the kingdom of heaven.

"Whoever receives one such child in My name receives Me, but whoever causes one of these little ones who believe in Me to sin, it would be better for him to have a great millstone fastened around his neck and to be drowned in the depth of the sea."

Matthew 18:2–6

Close of the Day

[Jesus said to them] "If your brother sins against you, go and tell him his fault, between you and him alone. If he listens to you, you have gained your brother. But if he does not listen, take one or two others along with you, that every charge may be established by the evidence of two or three witnesses. If he refuses to listen to them, tell it to the church. And if he refuses to listen even to the church, let him be to you as a Gentile and a tax collector. Truly, I say to you, whatever you bind on earth shall be bound in heaven, and whatever you loose on earth shall be loosed in heaven. Again I say to you, if two of you agree on earth about anything they ask, it will be done for them by My Father in heaven. For where two or three are gathered in My name, there am I among them."

Then Peter came up and said to Him, "Lord, how often will my brother sin against me, and I forgive him? As many as seven times?" Jesus said to him, "I do not say to you seven times, but seventy times seven.

"Therefore the kingdom of heaven may be compared to a king who wished to settle accounts with his servants. When he began to settle, one was brought to him who owed him ten thousand talents. And since he could not pay, his master ordered him to be sold, with his wife and children and all that he had, and payment to be made. So the servant fell on his knees, imploring him, 'Have patience with me, and I will pay you every-thing.' And out of pity for him, the master of that servant released him and forgave him the debt. But when that same servant went out, he found one of his fellow servants who owed him a hun-dred denarii, and seizing him, he began to choke him, saying, 'Pay what you owe.' So his fellow servant fell down and pleaded with him, 'Have patience with me, and I will pay you.' He refused and went and put him in prison until he should pay the debt. When his fellow servants saw what had taken place, they were greatly distressed, and they went and reported to their master all that had taken place. Then his master summoned him and said to him, 'You wicked servant! I forgave you all that debt because you pleaded with me. And should not you have had mercy on your fel-low servant, as I had mercy on you?' And in anger his master delivered him to the jailers, until he should pay all his debt. So also My heav-enly Father will do to every one of you, if you do not forgive your brother from your heart."

Matthew 18:15–35

Marriage

[Jesus] answered, "Have you not read that He who created them from the beginning made them male and female, and said, 'Therefore a man shall leave his father and his mother and hold fast to his wife, and they shall become one flesh'? So they are no longer two but one flesh. What therefore God has joined together, let not man separate."

Matthew 19:4–6

Morning Prayer

[Jesus told them this parable,] "For the kingdom of heaven is like a master of a house who went out early in the morning to hire laborers for his vineyard. After agreeing with the laborers for a denarius a day, he sent them into his vineyard. And going out about the third hour he saw others standing idle in the marketplace, and to them he said, 'You go into the vineyard too, and whatever is right I will give you.' So they went. Going out again about the sixth hour and the ninth hour, he did the same. And about the eleventh hour he went out and found others standing. And he said to them, 'Why do you stand here idle all day?' They said to him, 'Because no one has hired us.'

He said to them, 'You go into the vineyard too.' And when evening came, the owner of the vineyard said to his foreman, 'Call the laborers and pay them their wages, beginning with the last, up to the first.' And when those hired about the eleventh hour came, each of them received a denarius. Now when those hired first came, they thought they would receive more, but each of them also received a denarius. And on receiving it they grumbled at the master of the house, saying, 'These last worked only one hour, and you have made them equal to us who have borne the burden of the day and the scorching heat.' But he replied to one of them, 'Friend, I am doing you no wrong. Did you not agree with me for a denarius? Take what belongs to you and go. I choose to give to this last worker as I give to you. Am I not allowed to do what I choose with what belongs to me? Or do you begrudge my generosity?' So the last will be first, and the first last."

Matthew 20:1–16

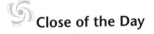

Close of the Day

[Jesus told them this parable,]"Then the kingdom of heaven will be like ten virgins who took their lamps and went to meet the bridegroom. Five of them were foolish, and five were wise. For when the foolish took their lamps, they took no oil with them, but the wise took flasks of oil with their lamps. As the bridegroom was delayed, they all became drowsy and slept. But at midnight there was a cry, 'Here is the bridegroom! Come out to meet him.' Then all those virgins rose and trimmed their lamps. And the foolish said to the wise, 'Give us some of your oil, for our lamps are going out.' But the wise answered, saying, 'Since there will not be enough for us and for you, go rather to the dealers and buy for yourselves.' And while they were going to buy, the bridegroom came, and those who were ready went in with him to the marriage feast, and the door was shut. Afterward the other virgins came also, saying, 'Lord, Lord, open to us.' But he answered, 'Truly, I say to you, I do not know you.' Watch therefore, for you know neither the day nor the hour."

Matthew 25:1–13

Early Evening

When it was evening, there came a rich man from Arimathea, named Joseph, who also was a disciple of Jesus. He went to Pilate and asked for the body of Jesus. Then Pilate ordered it to be given to him. And Joseph took the body and wrapped it in a clean linen shroud and laid it in his own new tomb, which he had cut in the rock. And he rolled a great stone to the entrance of the tomb and went away.

Matthew 27:57–60

 **Loneliness**

[Jesus said,] "Behold, I am with you always, to the end of the age."

Matthew 28:20b

 Prayer

[Jesus spoke to them saying,] "Therefore I tell you, whatever you ask in prayer, believe that you have received it, and it will be yours. And whenever you stand praying, forgive, if you have anything against anyone, so that your Father also who is in heaven may forgive you your trespasses. But if you do not forgive, neither will your Father who is in heaven forgive your trespasses."

Mark 11:24–26

 **Noon Prayer**

[Jesus spoke to them saying,] "But be on guard; I have told you all things beforehand. But in those days, after that tribulation, the sun will be darkened, and the moon will not give its light, and the stars will be falling from heaven, and the powers in the heavens will be shaken. And then they will see the Son of Man coming in clouds with great power and glory. And then He will send out the angels and gather His elect from the four winds, from the ends of the earth to the ends of heaven."

Mark 13:23–27

Morning Prayer

[Jesus spoke to them saying,] "But concerning that day or that hour, no one knows, not even the angels in heaven, nor the Son, but only the Father. Be on guard, keep awake. For you do not know when the time will come. It is like a man going on a journey, when he leaves home and puts his servants in charge, each with his work, and commands the doorkeeper to stay awake. Therefore stay awake—for you do not know when the master of the house will come, in the evening, or at midnight, or when the cock crows, or in the morning— lest he come suddenly and find you asleep. And what I say to you I say to all: Stay awake."

Mark 13:32–37

The Birth of Jesus

In those days a decree went out from Caesar Augustus that all the world should be registered.

This was the first registration when Quirinius was governor of Syria. And all went to be registered, each to his own town. And Joseph also went up from Galilee, from the town of Nazareth, to Judea, to the city of David, which is called Bethlehem, because he was of the house and lineage of David, to be registered with Mary, his betrothed, who was with child. And while they were there, the time came for her to give birth. And she gave birth to her firstborn son and wrapped him in swaddling cloths and laid him in a manger, because there was no place for them in the inn.

And in the same region there were shepherds out in the field, keeping watch over their flock by night. And an angel of the LORD appeared to them, and the glory of the LORD shone around them, and they were filled with fear. And the angel said to them, "Fear not, for behold, I bring you good news of a great joy that will be for all the people. For unto you is born this day in the city of David a Savior, who is Christ the LORD. And this will be a sign for you: you will find a baby wrapped in swaddling cloths and lying in a manger." And suddenly there was with the angel a multitude of the heavenly host praising God and saying,

"Glory to God in the highest,
and on earth peace among those with whom

He is pleased!"

When the angels went away from them into heaven, the shepherds said to one another, "Let us go over to Bethlehem and see this thing that has happened, which the LORD has made known to us." And they went with haste and found Mary and Joseph, and the baby lying in a manger. And when they saw it, they made known the saying that had been told them concerning this child. And all who heard it wondered at what the shepherds told them. But Mary treasured up all these things, pondering them in her heart. And the shepherds returned, glorifying and praising God for all they had heard and seen, as it had been told them.

Luke 2:1–20

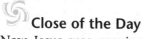

Close of the Day

Now Jesus was praying in a certain place, and when He finished, one of His disciples said to Him, "LORD, teach us to pray, as John taught his disciples." And He said to them, "When you pray, say:

"Father, hallowed be your name.

Your kingdom come.

Give us each day our daily bread,

and forgive us our sins,

as we forgive everyone who [sins against] us.

And lead us not into temptation."

And He said to them, "Which of you who has a

friend will go to him at midnight and say to him, 'Friend, lend me three loaves, for a friend of mine has arrived on a journey, and I have nothing to set before him'; and he will answer from within, 'Do not bother me; the door is now shut, and my children are with me in bed. I cannot get up and give you anything'? I tell you, though he will not get up and give him anything because he is his friend, yet because of his impudence he will rise and give him whatever he needs. And I tell you, ask, and it will be given to you; seek, and you will find; knock, and it will be opened to you. For everyone who asks receives, and the one who seeks finds, and to the one who knocks it will be opened. What father among you, if his son asks for a fish, will instead of a fish give him a serpent; or if he asks for an egg, will give him a scorpion? If you then, who are evil, know how to give good gifts to your children, how much more will the heavenly Father give the Holy Spirit to those who ask Him!"

Luke 11:1–13

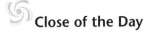

Close of the Day

Someone in the crowd said to [Jesus], "Teacher, tell my brother to divide the inheritance with me." But He said to him, "Man, who made Me a judge or arbitrator over you?" And He said to them, "Take care, and be on your guard against all covetousness, for one's life does not consist in the abundance of his possessions." And He told them a parable, saying, "The land of a rich man produced plentifully, and he thought to himself, 'What shall I do, for I have nowhere to store my crops?' And he said, 'I will do this: I will tear down my barns and build larger ones, and there I will store all my grain and my goods. And I will say to my soul, Soul, you have ample goods laid up for many years; relax, eat, drink, be merry.' But God said to him, 'Fool! This night your soul is required of you, and the things you have prepared, whose will they be?' So is the one who lays up treasure for himself and is not rich toward God."

And He said to His disciples, "Therefore I tell you, do not be anxious about your life, what you will eat, nor about your body, what you will put on. For life is more than food, and the body more than clothing. Consider the ravens: they neither sow nor reap, they have neither storehouse nor barn, and yet God feeds them. Of how much more value are you than the birds! And which of you by being anxious can add a single hour to his span of life? If then you are not able to do as small a thing as that, why are you anxious about the rest? Consider the lilies, how they grow: they neither toil nor spin, yet I tell you, even Solomon in all his glory was not arrayed like one of these.

But if God so clothes the grass, which is alive in the field today, and tomorrow is thrown into the oven, how much more will He clothe you, O you of little faith! And do not seek what you are to eat and what you are to drink, nor be worried. For all the nations of the world seek after these things, and your Father knows that you need them. Instead, seek His kingdom, and these things will be added to you.

"Fear not, little flock, for it is your Father's good pleasure to give you the kingdom. Sell your possessions, and give to the needy. Provide yourselves with moneybags that do not grow old, with a treasure in the heavens that does not fail, where no thief approaches and no moth destroys. For where your treasure is, there will your heart be also."

Luke 12:13–34

 Evening Prayer

When one of those who reclined at table with [Jesus] heard these things, He said to him, "Blessed is everyone who will eat bread in the kingdom of God!" But [Jesus] said to him, "A man once gave a great banquet and invited many. And at the time for the banquet he sent his servant to say to those who had been invited, 'Come, for everything is now ready.' But they all alike began to make excuses. The first said to him, 'I have bought a field, and I must go out and see it. Please have me excused.' And another said, 'I have bought five yoke of oxen, and I go to examine them. Please have me excused.' And another said, 'I have married a wife, and therefore I cannot come.' So the servant came and reported these things to his master. Then the master of the house became angry and said to his servant, 'Go out quickly to the streets and lanes of the city, and bring in the poor and crippled and blind and lame.' And the servant said, 'Sir, what you commanded has been done, and still there is room.' And the master said to the servant, 'Go out to the highways and hedges and compel people to come in, that my house may be filled. For I tell you, none of those men who were invited shall taste my banquet.'"

Luke 14:15–24

Witnessing

[Jesus said to them,] "This will be your opportunity to bear witness. Settle it therefore in your minds not to meditate beforehand how to answer, for I will give you a mouth and wisdom, which none of your adversaries will be able to withstand or contradict."

Luke 21:13–15

Noon Prayer

It was now about the sixth hour, and there was darkness over the whole land until the ninth hour, while the sun's light failed. And the curtain of the temple was torn in two. Then Jesus, calling out with a loud voice, said, "Father, into Your hands I commit My spirit!" And having said this He breathed his last.

Luke 23:44–46

Morning Prayer; The Resurrection of Jesus

But on the first day of the week, at early dawn, they went to [Jesus'] tomb, taking the spices they had prepared. And they found the stone rolled away from the tomb, but when they went in they did not find the body of the LORD Jesus. While they were perplexed about this, behold, two men stood by them in dazzling apparel. And as they were frightened and bowed their faces to the ground, the men said to them, "Why do you seek the living among the dead? He is not here, but has risen. Remember how He told you, while He was still in Galilee, that the Son of Man must be delivered into the hands of sinful men and be crucified and on the third day rise." And they remembered His words.

Luke 24:1–8

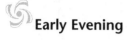 **Early Evening**

So they drew near to the village to which they were going. [The LORD] acted as if He were going farther, but they urged Him strongly, saying, "Stay with us, for it is toward evening and the day is now far spent." So He went in to stay with them. When He was at table with them, He took the bread and blessed and broke it and gave it to them. And their eyes were opened, and they recognized Him. And He vanished from their sight.

Luke 24:28–31

 Love; Salvation

[Jesus spoke to them saying,] "No one has ascended into heaven except He who descended from heaven, the Son of Man. And as Moses lifted up the serpent in the wilderness, so must the Son of Man be lifted up, that whoever believes in Him may have eternal life. For God so loved the world, that He gave His only Son, that whoever believes in Him should not perish but have eternal life. For God did not send His Son into the world to condemn the world, but in order that the world might be saved through Him. Whoever believes in Him is not condemned, but whoever does not believe is condemned already, because he has not believed in the name of the only Son of God. And this is the judgment: the light has come into the world, and people loved the darkness rather than the light because their deeds were evil. For everyone who does wicked things hates the light and does not come to the light, lest his deeds should be exposed. But whoever does what is true comes to the light, so that it may be clearly seen that his deeds have been carried out in God."

John 3:13–21

Early Evening

When they found Him on the other side of the sea, they said to Him, "Rabbi, when did You come here?" Jesus answered them, "Truly, truly, I say to you, you are seeking Me, not because you saw signs, but because you ate your fill of the loaves. Do not labor for the food that perishes, but for the food that endures to eternal life, which the Son of Man will give to you. For on Him God the Father has set His seal." Then they said to Him, "What must we do, to be doing the works of God?" Jesus answered them, "This is the work of God, that you believe in Him whom He has sent." So they said to Him, "Then what sign do you do, that we may see and believe You? What work do You perform? Our fathers ate the manna in the wilderness; as it is written, 'He gave them bread from heaven to eat.'" Jesus then said to them, "Truly, truly, I say to you, it was not Moses who gave you the bread from heaven, but My Father gives you the true bread from heaven. For the bread of God is He who comes down from heaven and gives life to the world." They said to Him, "Sir, give us this bread always."

Jesus said to them, "I am the bread of life; whoever comes to Me shall not hunger, and whoever believes in Me shall never thirst."

John 6:25–35

Early Evening

So Jesus again said to them, "Truly, truly, I say to you, I am the door of the sheep. All who came before Me are thieves and robbers, but the sheep did not listen to them. I am the door. If anyone enters by Me, he will be saved and will go in and out and find pasture. The thief comes only to steal and kill and destroy. I came that they may have life and have it abundantly. I am the good shepherd. The good shepherd lays down his life for the sheep. He who is a hired hand and not a shepherd, who does not own the sheep, sees the wolf coming and leaves the sheep and flees, and the wolf snatches them and scatters them. He flees because he is a hired hand and cares nothing for the sheep. I am the good shepherd. I know My own and My own know Me, just as the Father knows Me and I know the Father; and I lay down My life for the sheep. And I have other sheep that are not of this fold. I must bring them also, and they will listen to My voice. So there will be one flock, one shepherd. For this reason the Father loves Me, because I lay down My life that I may take it up again. No one takes it from Me, but I lay it down of My own accord. I have authority to lay it down, and I have authority to take it up again. This charge I have received from My Father."

John 10:7–18

 ## Salvation

"Let not your hearts be troubled [said Jesus]. Believe in God; believe also in Me. In My Father's house are many rooms. If it were not so, would I have told you that I go to prepare a place for you? And if I go and prepare a place for you, I will come again and will take you to Myself, that where I am you may be also. And you know the way to where I am going." Thomas said to Him, "LORD, we do not know where You are going. How can we know the way?" Jesus said to him, "I am the way, and the truth, and the life. No one comes to the Father except through Me."

John 14:1–6

Noon Prayer

[Jesus spoke to them saying,] "I am the true vine, and My Father is the vinedresser. Every branch of Mine that does not bear fruit He takes away, and every branch that does bear fruit He prunes, that it may bear more fruit. Already you are clean because of the word that I have spoken to you. Abide in Me, and I in you. As the branch cannot bear fruit by itself, unless it abides in the vine, neither can you, unless you abide in me. I am the vine; you are the branches. Whoever abides in Me and I in him, he it is that bears much fruit, for apart from Me you can do nothing. If anyone does not abide in Me he is thrown away like a branch and withers; and the branches are gathered, thrown into the fire, and burned. If you abide in Me, and My words abide in you, ask whatever you wish, and it will be done for you. By this My Father is glorified, that you bear much fruit and so prove to be My disciples. As the Father has loved Me, so have I loved you. Abide in My love."

John 15:1–9

 **Protection**

[Jesus prayed saying,] "I am no longer in the world, but they are in the world, and I am coming to you. Holy Father, keep them in Your name, which You have given Me, that they may be one, even as We are one. While I was with them, I kept them in Your name, which You have given Me. I have guarded them, and not one of them has been lost except the son of destruction, that the Scripture might be fulfilled. But now I am coming to You, and these things I speak in the world, that they may have My joy fulfilled in themselves. I have given them Your Word, and the world has hated them because they are not of the world, just as I am not of the world. I do not ask that You take them out of the world, but that You keep them from the evil one."

John 17:11–15

 The Death and Burial of Jesus

So [Pilate] delivered [Jesus] over to them to be crucified.

So they took Jesus, and He went out, bearing His own cross, to the place called the place of a skull, which in Aramaic is called Golgotha. There they

111

crucified Him, and with Him two others, one on either side, and Jesus between them. Pilate also wrote an inscription and put it on the cross. It read, "Jesus of Nazareth, the King of the Jews." Many of the Jews read this inscription, for the place where Jesus was crucified was near the city, and it was written in Aramaic, in Latin, and in Greek. So the chief priests of the Jews said to Pilate, "Do not write, 'The King of the Jews,' but rather, 'This man said, I am King of the Jews.'" Pilate answered, "What I have written I have written."

When the soldiers had crucified Jesus, they took His garments and divided them into four parts, one part for each soldier; also His tunic. But the tunic was seamless, woven in one piece from top to bottom, so they said to one another, "Let us not tear it, but cast lots for it to see whose it shall be." This was to fulfill the Scripture which says,

> "They divided My garments among them,
> and for My clothing they cast lots."

So the soldiers did these things, but standing by the cross of Jesus were His mother and His mother's sister, Mary the wife of Clopas, and Mary Magdalene. When Jesus saw His mother and the disciple whom He loved standing nearby, He said to His mother, "Woman, behold, your son!" Then He said to the disciple, "Behold, your mother!" And from that hour the disciple took her to his own home.

After this, Jesus, knowing that all was now finished, said (to fulfill the Scripture), "I thirst." A jar full of sour wine stood there, so they put a sponge full of the sour wine on a hyssop branch and held it to His mouth. When Jesus had received the sour wine, He said, "It is finished," and He bowed His head and gave up His spirit.

Since it was the day of Preparation, and so that the bodies would not remain on the cross on the Sabbath (for that Sabbath was a high day), the Jews asked Pilate that their legs might be broken and that they might be taken away. So the soldiers came and broke the legs of the first, and of the other who had been crucified with him. But when they came to Jesus and saw that He was already dead, they did not break His legs. But one of the soldiers pierced His side with a spear, and at once there came out blood and water. He who saw it has borne witness—his testimony is true, and he knows that he is telling the truth—that you also may believe. For these things took place that the Scripture might be fulfilled: "Not one of His bones will be broken." And again another Scripture says, "They will look on Him whom they have pierced."

After these things Joseph of Arimathea, who was a disciple of Jesus, but secretly for fear of the Jews, asked Pilate that he might take away the body of Jesus, and Pilate gave him permission. So he came and took away His body. Nicodemus also, who earlier had come to Jesus by night, came bringing a mixture of myrrh and aloes, about seventy-five pounds in weight. So they took the body of Jesus and bound it in linen cloths with the spices, as is the burial custom of the Jews. Now in the place where He was crucified there was a garden, and in the garden a new tomb in which no one had yet been laid. So because of the Jewish day of Preparation, since the tomb was close at hand, they laid Jesus there.

John 19:16–42

Morning Prayer

Just as day was breaking, Jesus stood on the shore; yet the disciples did not know that it was Jesus. Jesus said to them, "Children, do you have any fish?" They answered Him, "No." He said to them, "Cast the net on the right side of the boat, and you will find some." So they cast it, and now they were not able to haul it in, because of the quantity of fish. That disciple whom Jesus loved therefore said to Peter, "It is the LORD!" When Simon Peter heard that it was the LORD, he put on his outer garment, for he was stripped for work, and threw himself into the sea. The other disciples came in the boat, dragging the net full of fish, for they were not far from the land, but about a hundred yards off.

When they got out on land, they saw a charcoal fire in place, with fish laid out on it, and bread. Jesus said to them, "Bring some of the fish that you have just caught." So Simon Peter went aboard and hauled the net ashore, full of large fish, 153 of them. And although there were so many, the net was not torn. Jesus said to them, "Come and have breakfast." Now none of the disciples dared ask Him, "Who are You?" They knew it was the LORD. Jesus came and took the bread and gave it to them, and so with the fish. This was now the third time that Jesus was revealed to the disciples after He was raised from the dead.

John 21:4–14

Witnessing; Salvation

For I am not ashamed of the gospel, for it is the power of God for salvation to everyone who believes, to the Jew first and also to the Greek. For in it the righteousness of God is revealed from faith for faith, as it is written, "The righteous shall live by faith."

Romans 1:16–17

Repentance

Therefore, since we have been justified by faith,

115

we have peace with God through our LORD Jesus Christ. Through Him we have also obtained access by faith into this grace in which we stand, and we rejoice in hope of the glory of God. More than that, we rejoice in our sufferings, knowing that suffering produces endurance, and endurance produces character, and character produces hope, and hope does not put us to shame, because God's love has been poured into our hearts through the Holy Spirit who has been given to us.

For while we were still weak, at the right time Christ died for the ungodly. For one will scarcely die for a righteous person—though perhaps for a good person one would dare even to die—but God shows His love for us in that while we were still sinners, Christ died for us.

Romans 5:1–8

 Morning Prayer

What shall we say then? Are we to continue in sin that grace may abound? By no means! How can we who died to sin still live in it? Do you not know that all of us who have been baptized into Christ Jesus were baptized into His death? We were buried therefore with Him by baptism into death, in order that, just as Christ was raised from the dead by the glory of the Father, we too might walk in newness of life.

Romans 6:1–4

 **Noon Prayer**

For I know that nothing good dwells in me, that is, in my flesh. For I have the desire to do what is right, but not the ability to carry it out. For I do not do the good I want, but the evil I do not want is what I keep on doing. Now if I do what I do not want, it is no longer I who do it, but sin that dwells within me.

So I find it to be a law that when I want to do right, evil lies close at hand. For I delight in the law of God, in my inner being, but I see in my members another law waging war against the law of my mind and making me captive to the law of sin that dwells in my members. Wretched man that I am! Who will deliver me from this body of death? Thanks be to God through Jesus Christ our Lord! So then, I myself serve the law of God with my mind, but with my flesh I serve the law of sin.

Romans 7:18–25

 Assurance; Close of Day

What then shall we say to these things? If God is

for us, who can be against us? He who did not spare His own Son but gave Him up for us all, how will He not also with Him graciously give us all things? Who shall bring any charge against God's elect? It is God who justifies. Who is to condemn? Christ Jesus is the one who died—more than that, who was raised—who is at the right hand of God, who indeed is interceding for us. Who shall separate us from the love of Christ? Shall tribulation, or distress, or persecution, or famine, or nakedness, or danger, or sword? As it is written,

> "For your sake we are being killed all the day long;
>
> we are regarded as sheep to be slaughtered."

No, in all these things we are more than conquerors through Him who loved us. For I am sure that neither death nor life, nor angels nor rulers, nor things present nor things to come, nor powers, nor height nor depth, nor anything else in all creation, will be able to separate us from the love of God in Christ Jesus our LORD.

Romans 8:31–39

 Noon Prayer

I appeal to you therefore, brothers, by the mercies of God, to present your bodies as a living sacrifice, holy and acceptable to God, which is your spiritual worship. Do not be conformed to this world, but be transformed by the renewal of your mind, that by testing you may discern what is the will of God, what is good and acceptable and perfect.

Romans 12:1–2

 Noon Prayer

Only let each person lead the life that the LORD has assigned to him, and to which God has called him. You were bought with a price; do not become slaves of men. So, brothers, in whatever condition each was called, there let him remain with God.

1 Corinthians 7:17a, 23–24

 Temptation

No temptation has overtaken you that is not common to man. God is faithful, and He will not let you be tempted beyond your ability, but with the temptation He will also provide the way of escape, that you may be able to endure it.

1 Corinthians 10:13

Love

If I speak in the tongues of men and of angels, but have not love, I am a noisy gong or a clanging cymbal. And if I have prophetic powers, and understand all mysteries and all knowledge, and if I have all faith, so as to remove mountains, but have not love, I am nothing. If I give away all I have, and if I deliver up my body to be burned, but have not love, I gain nothing.

Love is patient and kind; love does not envy or boast; it is not arrogant or rude. It does not insist on its own way; it is not irritable or resentful; it does not rejoice at wrongdoing, but rejoices with the truth. Love bears all things, believes all things, hopes all things, endures all things.

Love never ends. As for prophecies, they will pass away; as for tongues, they will cease; as for knowledge, it will pass away. For we know in part and we prophesy in part, but when the perfect comes, the partial will pass away. When I was a child, I spoke like a child, I thought like a child, I reasoned like a child. When I became a man, I gave up childish ways. For now we see in a mirror dimly, but then face to face. Now I know in part; then I shall know fully, even as I have been fully known.

So now faith, hope, and love abide, these three; but the greatest of these is love.

1 Corinthians 13

Grief

Behold! I tell you a mystery. We shall not all sleep, but we shall all be changed, in a moment, in the twinkling of an eye, at the last trumpet. For the trumpet will sound, and the dead will be raised imperishable, and we shall be changed. For this perishable body must put on the imperishable, and this mortal body must put on immortality. When the perishable puts on the imperishable, and the mortal puts on immortality, then shall come to pass the saying that is written:

"Death is swallowed up in victory."
"O death, where is your victory?
O death, where is your sting?"

The sting of death is sin, and the power of sin is the law. But thanks be to God, who gives us the victory through our LORD Jesus Christ.

1 Corinthians 15:51–57

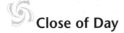 **Close of Day**

So we do not lose heart. Though our outer nature is wasting away, our inner nature is being renewed day by day. For this slight momentary affliction is preparing for us an eternal weight of glory beyond all comparison, as we look not to

121

the things that are seen but to the things that are unseen. For the things that are seen are transient, but the things that are unseen are eternal.

2 Corinthians 4:16–18

 Love

But God, being rich in mercy, because of the great love with which He loved us, even when we were dead in our trespasses, made us alive together with Christ—by grace you have been saved.

Ephesians 2:4–5

 Salvation

For by grace you have been saved through faith. And this is not your own doing; it is the gift of God, not a result of works, so that no one may boast.

Ephesians 2:8–9

 Morning Prayer

Now this I say and testify in the LORD, that you must no longer walk as the Gentiles do, in the futility of their minds. They are darkened in their understanding, alienated from the life of God because of the ignorance that is in them, due to their hardness of heart. They have become callous and have given themselves up to sensuality, greedy to practice every kind of impurity. But that is not the way you learned Christ!— assuming that you have heard about Him and were taught in Him, as the truth is in Jesus, to put off your old self, which belongs to your former manner of life and is corrupt through deceitful desires, and to be renewed in the spirit of your minds, and to put on the new self, created after the likeness of God in true righteousness and holiness.

Ephesians 4:17–24

Friendship

Let no corrupting talk come out of your mouths, but only such as is good for building up, as fits the occasion, that it may give grace to those who hear. And do not grieve the Holy Spirit of God, by whom you were sealed for the day of redemption. Let all bitterness and wrath and anger and clamor and slander be put away from you, along with all malice. Be kind to one another, tenderhearted, forgiving one another, as God in Christ forgave you.

Ephesians 4:29–32

Christian Life; Love

Therefore be imitators of God, as beloved children. And walk in love, as Christ loved us and gave Himself up for us, a fragrant offering and sacrifice to God.

But sexual immorality and all impurity or covetousness must not even be named among you, as is proper among saints. Let there be no filthiness nor foolish talk nor crude joking, which are out of place, but instead let there be thanksgiving.

Ephesians 5:1–4

 Marriage

Wives, submit to your own husbands, as to the LORD. For the husband is the head of the wife even as Christ is the head of the church, His body, and is Himself its Savior. Now as the church submits to Christ, so also wives should submit in everything to their husbands.

Husbands, love your wives, as Christ loved the church and gave Himself up for her, that He might sanctify her, having cleansed her by the washing of water with the word, so that He might present the church to Himself in splendor, without spot or wrinkle or any such thing, that she might be holy and without blemish. In the same way husbands should love their wives as their own bodies. He who loves his wife loves himself. For no one ever hated his own flesh, but nourishes and cherishes it, just as Christ does the church, because we are members of His body. "Therefore a man shall leave his father and mother and hold fast to his wife, and the two shall become one flesh." This mystery is profound, and I am saying that it refers to Christ and the church. However, let each one of you love his wife as himself, and let the wife see that she respects her husband.

Ephesians 5:22–33

Encouragement; Evening Prayer

Finally, be strong in the LORD and in the strength of His might. Put on the whole armor of God, that you may be able to stand against the schemes of the devil. For we do not wrestle against flesh and blood, but against the rulers, against the authorities, against the cosmic powers over this present darkness, against the spiritual forces of evil in the heavenly places. Therefore take up the whole armor of God, that you may be able to withstand in the evil day, and having done all, to stand firm. Stand therefore, having fastened on the belt of truth, and having put on the breastplate of righteousness, and, as shoes for your feet, having put on the readiness given by the gospel of peace. In all circumstances take up the shield of faith, with which you can extinguish all the flaming darts of the evil one; and take the helmet of salvation, and the sword of the Spirit, which is the word of God, praying at all times in the Spirit, with all prayer and supplication. To that end keep alert with all perseverance, making supplication for all the saints.

Ephesians 6:10–18

 Morning Prayer

If then you have been raised with Christ, seek the things that are above, where Christ is, seated at the right hand of God. Set your minds on things that are above, not on things that are on earth. For you have died, and your life is hidden with Christ in God. When Christ who is your life appears, then you also will appear with Him in glory.

Colossians 3:1–4

Work

Whatever you do, work heartily, as for the LORD and not for men, knowing that from the LORD you will receive the inheritance as your reward. You are serving the LORD Christ.

Colossians 3:23, 24

 Grief

But we do not want you to be uninformed, brothers, about those who are asleep, that you may not grieve as others do who have no hope. For since we believe that Jesus died and rose again, even so, through Jesus, God will bring with Him those who have fallen asleep. For this we declare to you by a word from the LORD, that we who are alive, who are left until the coming of the LORD, will not precede those who have fallen asleep. For the LORD Himself will descend from heaven with a cry of command, with the voice of an archangel, and with the sound of the trumpet of God. And the dead in Christ will rise first. Then we who are alive, who are left, will be caught up together with them in the clouds to meet the LORD in the air, and so we will always be with the LORD. Therefore encourage one another with these words.

1 Thessalonians 4:13–18

Widow

She who is truly a widow, left all alone, has set her hope on God and continues in supplications and prayers night and day.

1 Timothy 5:5

Money

Now there is great gain in godliness with contentment, for we brought nothing into the world, and we cannot take anything out of the world. But if we have food and clothing, with these we will be content. But those who desire to be rich fall into temptation, into a snare, into many senseless and harmful desires that plunge people into ruin and destruction. For the love of money is a root of all kinds of evils. It is through this craving that some have wandered away from the faith and pierced themselves with many pangs.

1 Timothy 6:6–10

Stress

Let your reasonableness be known to everyone. The LORD is at hand; do not be anxious about anything, but in everything by prayer and supplication with thanksgiving let your requests be made known to God. And the peace of God, which surpasses all understanding, will guard your hearts and your minds in Christ Jesus.

Philippians 4:5–7

Encouragement

Therefore do not throw away your confidence, which has a great reward. For you have need of endurance, so that when you have done the will of God you may receive what is promised.

Hebrews 10:35–36

Encouragement

Therefore, since we are surrounded by so great a cloud of witnesses, let us also lay aside every weight, and sin which clings so closely, and let us run with endurance the race that is set before us, looking to Jesus, the founder and perfecter of our faith, who for the joy that was set before Him endured the cross, despising the shame, and is seated at the right hand of the throne of God.

Consider Him who endured from sinners such hostility against Himself, so that you may not grow weary or fainthearted. In your struggle against sin you have not yet resisted to the point of shedding your blood. And have you forgotten the exhortation that addresses you as sons?

"My son, do not regard lightly the discipline of the LORD, nor be weary when reproved by Him.

For the LORD disciplines the one He loves, and chastises every son whom He receives."

It is for discipline that you have to endure. God is treating you as sons. For what son is there whom his father does not discipline? If you are left without discipline, in which all have participated, then you are illegitimate children and not sons. Besides this, we have had earthly fathers who disciplined us and we respected them. Shall we not much more be subject to the Father of spirits and live? For they disciplined us for a short time as it seemed best to them, but He disciplines us for our good, that we may share His holiness. For the moment all discipline seems painful rather than pleasant, but later it yields the peaceful fruit of righteousness to those who have been trained by it.

Hebrews 12:1–11

 Encouragement; Noon Prayer

Blessed be the God and Father of our LORD Jesus Christ! According to His great mercy, He has caused us to be born again to a living hope through the resurrection of Jesus Christ from the dead, to an inheritance that is imperishable, undefiled, and unfading, kept in heaven for you, who by God's power are being guarded through faith for a salvation ready to be revealed in the last time. In this you rejoice, though now for a little while, if necessary, you have been grieved by various trials, so that the tested genuineness of your faith—more precious than gold that perishes though it is tested by fire—may be found to result in praise and glory and honor at the revelation of Jesus Christ. Though you have not seen Him, you love Him. Though you do not now see Him, you believe in Him and rejoice with joy that is inexpressible and filled with glory, obtaining the outcome of your faith, the salvation of your souls.

1 Peter 1:3–9

 Sin

If we say we have fellowship with Him while we walk in darkness, we lie and do not practice the truth. But if we walk in the light, as He is in the light, we have fellowship with one another, and the blood of Jesus His Son cleanses us from all sin. If we say we have no sin, we deceive ourselves, and the truth is not in us. If we confess our sins, He is faithful and just to forgive us our sins and to cleanse us from all unrighteousness.

1 John 1:6–9

Peace

See what kind of love the Father has given to us, that we should be called children of God; and so we are. The reason why the world does not know us is that it did not know Him. Beloved, we are God's children now, and what we will be has not yet appeared; but we know that when He appears we shall be like Him, because we shall see Him as He is.

1 John 3:1–2

 Love; Salvation

Beloved, let us love one another, for love is from God, and whoever loves has been born of God and knows God. Anyone who does not love does not know God, because God is love. In this the love of God was made manifest among us, that God sent His only Son into the world, so that we might live through Him. In this is love, not that we have loved God but that He loved us and sent His Son to be the propitiation for our sins.

1 John 4:7–10

Christian Life

But you, beloved, build yourselves up in your most holy faith; pray in the Holy Spirit; keep yourselves in the love of God, waiting for the mercy of our LORD Jesus Christ that leads to eternal life. And have mercy on those who doubt; save others by snatching them out of the fire; to others show mercy with fear, hating even the garment stained by the flesh.

Now to Him who is able to keep you from stumbling and to present you blameless before the presence of His glory with great joy, to the only God, our Savior, through Jesus Christ our LORD, be glory, majesty, dominion, and authority, before all time and now and forever. Amen.

Jude 20–25

Close of the Day

And I saw no temple in the city, for its temple is the LORD God the Almighty and the Lamb. And the city has no need of sun or moon to shine on it, for the glory of God gives it light, and its lamp is the Lamb. By its light will the nations walk, and the kings of the earth will bring their glory into it, and its gates will never be shut by day— and there will be no night there. They will bring into it the glory and the honor of the nations. But nothing unclean will ever enter it, nor anyone who does what is detestable or false, but only those who are written in the Lamb's book of life.

Then the angel showed me the river of the water of life, bright as crystal, flowing from the throne of God and of the Lamb through the middle of the street of the city; also, on either side of the river, the tree of life with its twelve kinds of fruit, yielding its fruit each month. The leaves of the tree were for the healing of the nations. No longer will there be anything accursed, but the throne of God and of the Lamb will be in it, and His servants will worship Him. They will see His face, and His name will be on their foreheads. And night will be no more. They will need no light of lamp or sun, for the LORD God will be their light, and they will reign forever and ever.

Revelation 21:22–22:5

Prayers for Ourselves
and Others

1.

General Prayer

O God almighty and merciful, let Your fatherly kindness be upon all whom You have made; hear the prayers of all who call upon You; open the eyes of those who never pray for themselves; pity the sighs of such as are in misery; deal mercifully with those who are in darkness; increase the number and graces of those who fear and serve You daily; preserve this land from the misfortunes of war, this church from all wild and dangerous errors, this people from forgetting You, their Lord and Benefactor; be gracious to all those countries that are made desolate by earthquakes, droughts, floods, epidemics, or persecution; bless all persons and places to which Your providence has made us debtors, all who have been instrumental to our good by their assistance, advice, example, or writings, and make us in our turn useful to others; let none of those who desire our prayers want for Your mercy, but defend and comfort and conduct them through to their life's end; through Jesus Christ, Your Son, our Lord. Amen.

2.

FOR ADVENT

Stir up our hearts, O Lord, to make ready the way of Your only-begotten Son, so that at His second coming we may worship Him in purity; through Jesus Christ, Your Son, our Lord. Amen.

3.

FOR CHRISTMAS EVE

O God, because You once caused this holy night to shine with the brightness of the true Light, grant that we who have known the mystery of that Light here on earth may come to the full measure of its joys in heaven; through Jesus Christ, Your Son, our Lord. Amen.

4.

FOR CHRISTMAS DAY

O almighty God, grant that the birth of Your only-begotten Son in human flesh may set us free, who in sin are held in bondage; through Jesus Christ, Your Son, our Lord. Amen.

5.

FOR EPIPHANY

O God, by the leading of a star You once

made known to all nations Your only-begotten Son; now lead us, who know You by faith, to know in heaven the fullness of Your divine goodness; through Jesus Christ, Your Son, our Lord. Amen.

6.

FOR LENT

Almighty and everlasting God, because You hate nothing You have made and forgive the sins of all who are penitent, create in us new and contrite hearts that we, worthily repenting our sins and acknowledging our wretchedness, may obtain from You, the God of all mercy, perfect remission and forgiveness; through Jesus Christ, Your Son, our Lord. Amen.

7.

FOR PALM SUNDAY

Almighty and everlasting God the Father, who sent Your Son to take our nature upon Him and to suffer death on the cross that all mankind should follow the example of His great humility, mercifully grant that we may both follow the example of our Savior Jesus Christ in His patience and also have our portion in His resurrection; through Jesus Christ, Your Son, our Lord. Amen.

8.

For Good Friday

Merciful and everlasting God, the Father, who did not spare Your only Son, but delivered Him up for us all that He might bear our sins on the cross, grant that our hearts may be so fixed with steadfast faith in our Savior that we may not fear the power of any adversaries; through Jesus Christ, Your Son, our Lord. Amen.

9.

For Easter

O God, for our redemption You have given Your only-begotten Son to the death of the cross, and by His glorious resurrection You have delivered us from the power of our enemy. Therefore grant that all our sin may be drowned through daily repentance and that day by day a new man may arise to live before You in righteousness and purity forever; through Jesus Christ, Your Son, our Lord. Amen.

10.

For Pentecost

O God, on this day You once taught the hearts of Your faithful people by sending them the light of Your Holy Spirit. Grant us in our day by the same Spirit to have a right understanding in all things and evermore to rejoice in His holy consolation; through Jesus Christ, Your Son, our Lord. Amen.

11.

FOR TRINITY

Almighty and everlasting God, since You have given us, Your servants, grace to acknowledge the glory of the eternal Trinity by the confession of a true faith, and to worship the true Unity in the power of Your divine majesty, keep us also steadfast in this true faith and worship, and defend us ever from all our adversaries; through Jesus Christ, Your Son, our Lord. Amen.

12.

FOR REFORMATION (OCTOBER 31)

Almighty God, gracious Lord, pour out Your Holy Spirit on Your faithful people. Keep them steadfast in Your grace and truth, protect and comfort them in all temptations, defend them against all enemies of Your Word, and bestow on the Church Your saving peace; through Jesus Christ, Your Son, our Lord. Amen.

13

THE LITANY

*When used in group settings, the responses are set in **bold type**.*

O Lord, **have mercy.** O Christ, **have mercy.** O Lord, **have mercy.** O Christ, **hear us.** God the Father, in heaven, **have mercy.** God the Son, Redeemer of the world, **have mercy.** God the Holy Spirit, **have mercy.** Be gracious to us. **Spare us, good Lord.** Be gracious to us. **Help us, good Lord.**

From all sin, from all error, from all evil: from the crafts and assaults of the devil; from sudden and evil death: from pestilence and famine; from war and bloodshed; from sedition and from rebellion: from lightning and tempest; from all calamity by fire and water; and from everlasting death: **Good Lord, deliver us.**

By the mystery of Your holy incarnation; by Your holy nativity: by Your baptism, fasting, and temptation; by Your agony and bloody sweat; by Your cross and Passion; by Your precious death and burial: by Your glorious resurrection and ascension; and by the coming of the Holy Spirit, the Comforter: **Help us, good Lord.**

In all time of our tribulation; in all time of our prosperity; in the hour of death; and in the day of judgment: **Help us, good Lord.** We poor sinners implore You **to hear us, O Lord.**

To rule and govern Your holy Christian Church; to preserve all pastors and ministers of Your Church in the true knowledge and understanding of Your wholesome Word and to sustain them in holy living: to put an end to all schisms and causes of offense; to bring into the way of truth all who have erred and are deceived: to beat down Satan under our feet; to send faithful laborers into Your harvest; and to accompany Your Word with Your grace and Spirit: **We implore You to hear us, good Lord.**

To raise those that fall and to strengthen those that stand; and to comfort and help the weak hearted and the distressed: **We implore You to hear us, good Lord.** To give to all peoples concord and peace; to preserve our land from discord and strife; to give our country Your protection in every time of need: to direct and defend our president and all in authority; to bless and protect our magistrates and all our people: to watch over and help all who are in danger, necessity, and tribulation; to protect and guide all who travel: to grant all women with child, and all mothers with infant children, increasing happiness in their blessings; to defend all orphans and widows and provide for them: to strengthen and keep all sick persons and young children; to free those in bondage; and to have mercy on us all: **We implore You to hear us, good Lord.**

To forgive our enemies, persecutors, and slanderers and to turn their hearts; to give and preserve to our use the kindly fruits of the earth; and graciously to hear our prayers: **We implore You to hear us, good Lord.** Lord Jesus Christ, Son of God, **we implore You to hear us.**

Christ, the Lamb of God, who takes away the sin of the world, **have mercy.** Christ, the Lamb of God, who takes away the sin of the world, **have mercy.** Christ, the Lamb of God, who takes away the sin of the world, **grant us Your peace.** O Christ, hear us. O Lord, have mercy. O Christ, **have mercy.** O Lord, **have mercy. Amen.**

14.

Before Travel

Lord God our Father, You kept Abraham and Sarah in safety throughout the days of their pilgrimage, You led the children of Israel through the midst of the sea, and by a star You led the Wise Men to the infant Jesus. Protect and guide us now in this time as we set out to travel, make our ways safe and our homecomings joyful, and bring us at last to our heavenly home; through Jesus Christ, Your Son, our Lord. Amen.

15.

FOR THE CHURCH

O God, our heavenly Father, who manifested Your love by sending Your only-begotten Son into the world that all might live through Him, pour Your Holy Spirit upon Your church that it may fulfill His command to preach the Gospel in every land; send forth, we implore You, laborers into Your harvest; defend them in all dangers and temptations and hasten the time when they and those whom they have brought to You will meet and rejoice before Your heavenly throne; through Jesus Christ, Your Son, our Lord. Amen.

16.

FOR CHILDREN

Lord Jesus Christ, we implore You, by the innocence and obedience of Your holy childhood and by Your reverence and love for little children, guard our children, preserve their innocence, strengthen them when ready to slip, recover the wandering, and remove all that may hinder them from being brought up in faith and love for You; through Jesus Christ, Your Son, our Lord. Amen.

17.

For Commerce

Almighty God, enlighten all merchants, tradesmen, and businessmen with the gift of Your Holy Spirit that they may consider not what the world would sanction but what Your law commands; prosper with Your blessing all who are thus striving to regulate their dealings by the rule of truth and love; and if difficulties compass them in the world, quicken within them such a desire of laying up treasure in heaven as may cause them to accept Your perfect will, teaching them so to use earthly things that they may become partakers of the true riches which cannot fail; through Jesus Christ, Your Son, our Lord. Amen.

18.

Confession and Deliverance

Almighty and merciful God, the Fountain of all goodness, who knows the thoughts of my heart, I confess unto You that I have sinned against You and am evil in Your sight; wash me I implore You from the stains of my past sins, and give me grace and power to put away all hurtful things, so that, being delivered from the bondage of sin, I may bring forth worthy fruits of repentance; O Eternal Light, shine into my heart; O Eternal Goodness, deliver me from evil; O Eternal

Power, be to me a support; eternal Wisdom, scatter the darkness of my ignorance; eternal Pity, have mercy upon me; grant unto me that with all my heart and mind and strength I may evermore seek Your face; and finally bring me in Your infinite mercy to Your holy presence; so strengthen my weakness that, following in the footsteps of Your blessed Son, I may obtain the promise of my Baptism and enter into Your promised joy; through the same Jesus Christ, Your Son, our Lord. Amen.

19.

CHRISTIAN LIFE

Direct us, O Lord, in all our actions by Your gracious favor, and further us with Your continual help that in all our works, begun, continued, and ended in Your name, we may glorify Your holy name and finally by Your mercy receive eternal life; through Jesus Christ, Your Son, our Lord. Amen.

20.

COURAGE

Lord God, You have called Your servants to ventures of which we cannot see the ending, by paths as yet untrodden, through perils unknown. Give us faith to go out with good courage, not knowing where we go but only that Your hand is leading us and Your love supporting us; through Jesus Christ, Your Son, our Lord. Amen.

21.

For Enemies

O almighty, everlasting God, through Your own Son, our blessed Lord, You have commanded us to love our enemies, to do good to those who hate us, and to pray for those who persecute us. We pray that by Your gracious visitation all our enemies may be led to true repentance and may have the same love and be of one accord and one mind and heart with us, and with Your whole Church; through Jesus Christ, Your Son, our Lord. Amen.

22.

For Forgiveness

Grant, merciful Lord, to Your faithful people pardon and peace, that having been set free from our bondage to sin, we may serve You with a quiet mind; through Jesus Christ, Your Son, our Lord, Amen.

23.

For the Future

O God, You make the minds of Your faithful to be of one will; therefore grant to Your people that they may love what You command and desire what You promise, that among the manifold changes of this age our hearts may ever be fixed where true joys are to be found; through Jesus Christ, Your Son, our Lord. Amen.

24.

FOR HOUSE/HOME

Bless, O Lord, this house and all who dwell in it, as You were pleased to bless the house of Abraham, Isaac, and Jacob, that within these walls may dwell an angel of light and that we who dwell together in it may receive the abundant dew of heavenly blessing and through Your tender mercy rejoice in peace and quietness; through Jesus Christ, Your Son, our Lord. Amen.

25.

FOR MEDICAL VOCATIONS

O Lord Jesus Christ, who has power of life and death, of health and of sickness, give power, wisdom, and gentleness to all Your minister spirits: all physicians and surgeons, nurses and watchers of the sick, that, always bearing Your presence with them, they may not only heal but bless and shine as lamps of hope in the darkest hours of distress and fear; through Jesus Christ, Your Son, our Lord. Amen.

26.

FOR MERCY

Almighty and everlasting God, always more ready to hear than we to pray and always ready to give more than we either desire or deserve, pour down upon us the abundance of Your mercy, forgiving us those things of which our conscience is afraid, and giving us those good things we are not worthy to ask but through the merits and mediation of Jesus Christ, Your Son, our Lord. Amen.

27.

FOR THE NATION

O God, our Refuge and Strength, who orders all things in heaven and earth, look upon this nation with Your mercy; remember not our iniquities or the iniquities of our forefathers, and do not take Your just vengeance for our sins; pour out on us and on all the people of this land the spirit of grace and supplication and join us together in piety, loyalty, and brotherly love; direct the counsels and strengthen the hands of all in authority for the repression of crime and violence, the maintenance of order and law and of public peace and safety; so that, leading quiet lives in all godliness and honesty, we may live to be Your people, and You may show Yourself to be our God and that we may bless and glorify You, our Defender and Deliverer; through Jesus Christ, Your Son, our Lord, Amen.

28.

FOR THE NON-CHRISTIAN

O God of all the nations of the earth, remember the multitudes of the non-Christians, who, though created in Your image, are perishing in their sin; and grant that by the prayers and labors of Your holy church they may be delivered from all superstitions and unbelief and brought to worship You; through Him who You have sent to be our Salvation, the Resurrection and the Life of all the faithful, Your Son, Jesus Christ, our Lord. Amen.

29.

FOR PEACE

Almighty and most merciful God, You bring us through suffering and death with our Lord Jesus Christ to enter with Him into eternal glory. Grant us grace at all time to acknowledge and accept Your holy and gracious will, to remain in true faith, and to find peace and joy in the resurrection of the dead, and of the glory of everlasting life; through Jesus Christ, Your Son, our Lord. Amen.

30.

FOR PROTECTION

Almighty God, because You know that we are set among so many and great dangers that by reason of the weakness of our fallen nature we cannot always stand upright, grant us Your strength and protection to support us in all dangers and carry us through all temptations; through Jesus Christ, Your Son, our Lord. Amen.

31.

SALVATION

O Lord Jesus Christ, Son of the living God, who at the sixth hour was lifted up on the cross for the redemption of the world and shed Your blood for the remission of our sins, grant that by the virtue and merit of Your most holy life, passion, and death we may enter into the gates of paradise with joy; for Your mercy's sake. Amen.

32.

Father of all mercy, You never fail to help those who call on You for help. Give strength and confidence to Your *(son/daughter)* in *(his/her)* time of great need that *(he/she)* may know that You are near and that underneath are Your everlasting arms. Grant that, resting in Your protection *(he/she)* may fear no evil, for You are with *(him/her)* to comfort and deliver *(him/her)*; through Jesus Christ, Your Son, our Lord. Amen.

33.

Lord God, heavenly Father, look with favor upon this Your redeemed child, forgive *(him/her)* all *(his/her)* sin, comfort *(him/her)* with the promise of resurrection to life everlasting; through Jesus Christ, Your Son, our Lord. Amen.

34.

Depart in peace, you ransomed soul. May God the Father almighty who created you; may God the Son who redeemed you with His blood, may God the Holy Spirit who sanctified you in the water of Holy Baptism, receive you into the company of the saints and angels who live in the light of His glory forevermore; through Jesus Christ, Your Son, our Lord. Amen.

35.

Grant, O Lord, that when we are tempted, we may resist the devil; that when we are worried, we may cast all our care upon You; that when we are weary, we may seek Your rest; and that in all things we may live this day to Your glory; through Jesus Christ, Your Son, our Lord. Amen.

36.

Almighty God, since You know that we are set in the midst of so many and great dangers that by reason of the frailty of our nature we cannot always stand upright, grant us such strength and protection as may support us in all dangers and carry us through all temptations; through Jesus Christ, Your Son, our Lord. Amen.

37.

FOR THOSE LIVING IN UNREPENTED SIN

Almighty Father who makes children for Himself through water and the Word, have pity on your children who have become so entangled in the things of this world they have lost sight of the mercy and forgiveness won for them on the cross of Your Son, Jesus Christ. Deliver them from the tyranny of their unrepented deeds, and move their hearts by Your Spirit to look to their Savior alone for salvation, comfort, and peace; through that same Jesus Christ, Your Son, our Lord. Amen.

38.

FOR THOSE WHO HAVE FORSAKEN THE FAITH

Almighty, merciful, and gracious God and Father, visit those who have forsaken the Christian faith and those who wandered from Your Word; reveal to them their error and bring them back from their wanderings, that they with singleness of heart, and taking pleasure in the pure truth of Your Word alone, may be made partakers of eternal life; through Jesus Christ, Your Son, our Lord. Amen.

39.

FOR THOSE WHO SUFFER

We implore You to hear us, O God, for all who are worn by illness, all who are wronged and oppressed, the weary and heavy-laden, the aged and the dying, the poor and the lonely, all who are suffering for righteousness' sake, that they may be strengthened by Your might, consoled by Your love, and cherished by Your Fatherly pity; through Jesus Christ, Your Son, our Lord. Amen.

40.

IN TIME OF WAR

Father of mercies and God of all comfort, look

in pity upon all who are suffering in this time of strife and the warfare of nations. Protect the defenseless, heal the wounded, console the anxious and bereaved, and receive to Yourself those who die in the Lord Jesus Christ. Turn the hearts of our enemies, we pray, and forgive both them and us for our share in the sin that has brought this anguish upon humankind. Open up to us a way of reconciliation and lead us into the path of peace; through Jesus Christ, Your Son, our Lord. Amen.

41.

FOR OUR WORK

Almighty God, heavenly Father, as You have taken my life and made it holy in the death of Your Son, Jesus Christ, so too take the labor of my hands into Your own holy hands to accomplish Your will. Strengthen me in my vocation that discouragement, anger, resentment, and covetousness do not overtake me, but that all I do may be pleasing in Your sight; through Jesus Christ, Your Son, our Lord. Amen.

This is the text of Dr. Martin Luther's Small Catechism, the most popular explanation of the central teachings of the Christian faith. It has been used by countless Christians of all denominations for almost 500 years.

The Ten Commandments

As the head of the family should teach them in a simple way to his household

The First Commandment
You shall have no other gods.
What does this mean? We should fear, love, and trust in God above all things.

The Second Commandment
You shall not misuse the name of the Lord your God.
What does this mean? We should fear and love God so that we do not curse, swear, use satanic arts, lie, or deceive by His name, but call upon it in every trouble, pray, praise, and give thanks.

The Third Commandment
Remember the Sabbath day by keeping it holy.

What does this mean? We should fear and love God so that we do not despise preaching and His Word, but hold it sacred and gladly hear and learn it.

The Fourth Commandment
Honor your father and your mother.

What does this mean? We should fear and love God so that we do not despise or anger our parents and other authorities, but honor them, serve and obey them, love and cherish them.

The Fifth Commandment
You shall not murder.

What does this mean? We should fear and love God so that we do not hurt or harm our neighbor in his body, but help and support him in every physical need.

The Sixth Commandment
You shall not commit adultery.

What does this mean? We should fear and love God so that we lead a sexually pure and decent life in what we say and do, and husband and wife love and honor each other.

The Seventh Commandment
You shall not steal.

What does this mean? We should fear and love God so that we do not take our neighbor's money or possessions, or get them in any dishonest way, but help him to improve and protect his possessions and income.

The Eighth Commandment
You shall not give false testimony against your neighbor.

What does this mean? We should fear and love God so that we do not tell lies about our neighbor, betray him, slander him, or hurt his reputation, but defend him, speak well of him, and explain everything in the kindest way.

The Ninth Commandment
You shall not covet your neighbor's house.

What does this mean? We should fear and love God so that we do not scheme to get our neighbor's inheritance or house, or get it in a way which only appears right, but help and be of service to him in keeping it.

The Tenth Commandment
You shall not covet your neighbor's wife, or his manservant or maidservant, his ox or donkey, or anything that belongs to your neighbor.

What does this mean? We should fear and love

God so that we do not entice or force away our neighbor's wife, workers, or animals, or turn them against him, but urge them to stay and do their duty.

[The text of the commandments is from Exodus 20:3, 7–8, 12–17.]

The Close of the Commandments

What does God say about all these commandments?

He says: "I, the Lord your God, am a jealous God, punishing the children for the sin of the fathers to the third and fourth generation of those who hate Me, but showing love to a thousand generations of those who love Me and keep My commandments." [Exodus 20:5–6]

What does this mean? God threatens to punish all who break these commandments. Therefore, we should fear His wrath and not do anything against them. But He promises grace and every blessing to all who keep these commandments. Therefore, we should also love and trust in Him and gladly do what He commands.

The Apostles' Creed

As the head of the family should teach it in a simple way to his household

The First Article

Creation

I believe in God, the Father Almighty, Maker of heaven and earth.

What does this mean? I believe that God has made me and all creatures; that He has given me my body and soul, eyes, ears, and all my members, my reason and all my senses, and still takes care of them.

He also gives me clothing and shoes, food and drink, house and home, wife and children, land, animals, and all I have. He richly and daily provides me with all that I need to support this body and life.

He defends me against all danger and guards and protects me from all evil.

All this He does only out of fatherly, divine goodness and mercy, without any merit or worthiness in me. For all this it is my duty to thank and praise, to serve and obey Him.

This is most certainly true.

— The Second Article —

Redemption

And in Jesus Christ, His only Son, our Lord, who was conceived by the Holy Spirit, born of the Virgin Mary, suffered under Pontius Pilate, was crucified, died and was buried. He descended into hell. The third day He rose again from the dead. He ascended into heaven and sits at the right hand of God the Father Almighty. From thence He will come to judge the living and the dead.

What does this mean? I believe that Jesus Christ, true God, begotten of the Father from eternity, and also true man, born of the Virgin Mary, is my Lord, who has redeemed me, a lost and condemned person, purchased and won me from all sins, from death, and from the power of the devil; not with gold or silver, but with His holy, precious blood and with His innocent suffering and death, that I may be His own and live under Him in His kingdom, and serve Him in everlasting righteousness, innocence, and blessedness, just as He is risen from the dead, lives and reigns to all eternity.

This is most certainly true.

— The Third Article —

Sanctification

I believe in the Holy Spirit, the holy Christian Church, the communion of saints, the forgiveness of sins, the resurrection of the body, and the life everlasting. Amen

What does this mean? I believe that I cannot by my own reason or strength believe in Jesus Christ, my Lord, or come to Him; but the Holy Spirit has called me by the Gospel, enlightened me with His gifts, sanctified and kept me in the true faith.

In the same way He calls, gathers, enlightens, and sanctifies the whole Christian Church on earth and keeps it with Jesus Christ in the one true faith.

In this Christian Church He daily and richly forgives all my sins and the sins of all believers.

On the Last Day He will raise me and all the dead, and give eternal life to me and all believers in Christ.

This is most certainly true.

The Lord's Prayer

As the head of the family should teach it in a simple way to his household

Our Father, who art in heaven, hallowed be Thy name, Thy kingdom come, Thy will be done on earth as it is in heaven. Give us this day our daily bread; and forgive us our trespasses as we forgive those who trespass against us; and lead us not into temptation, but deliver us from evil. For Thine is the kingdom and the power and the glory forever and ever. Amen.

The Introduction

Our Father who art in heaven.

What does this mean? With these words God tenderly invites us to believe that He is our true Father and that we are His true children, so that with all boldness and confidence we may ask Him as dear children ask their dear father.

The First Petition

Hallowed be Thy name.

What does this mean? God's name is certainly holy in itself, but we pray in this petition that it may be kept holy among us also.

How is God's name kept holy? God's name is

kept holy when the Word of God is taught in its truth and purity, and we, as the children of God, also lead holy lives according to it. Help us to do this, dear Father in heaven! But anyone who teaches or lives contrary to God's Word profanes the name of God among us. Protect us from this, heavenly Father!

The Second Petition

Thy kingdom come.

What does this mean? The kingdom of God certainly comes by itself without our prayer, but we pray in this petition that it may come to us also.

How does God's kingdom come? God's kingdom comes when our heavenly Father gives us His Holy Spirit, so that by His grace we believe His holy Word and lead godly lives here in time and there in eternity.

The Third Petition

Thy will be done on earth as it is in heaven.

What does this mean? The good and gracious will of God is done even without our prayer, but we pray in this petition that it may be done among us also.

How is God's will done? God's will is done when He breaks and hinders every evil plan and purpose of the devil, the world, and our sinful nature, which do not want us to hallow God's name or let His kingdom come; and when He strengthens and keeps us firm in His Word and faith until we die.

This is His good and gracious will.

The Fourth Petition

Give us this day our daily bread.

What does this mean? God certainly gives daily bread to everyone without our prayers, even to all evil people, but we pray in this petition that God would lead us to realize this and to receive our daily bread with thanksgiving.

What is meant by daily bread? Daily bread includes everything that has to do with the support and needs of the body, such as food, drink, clothing, shoes, house, home, land, animals, money, goods, a devout husband or wife, devout children, devout workers, devout and faithful rulers, good government, good weather, peace, health, self-control, good reputation, good friends, faithful neighbors, and the like.

⚜ The Fifth Petition ⚜

And forgive us our trespasses
as we forgive those who trespass against us.

What does this mean? We pray in this petition that our Father in heaven would not look at our sins, or deny our prayer because of them. We are neither worthy of the things for which we pray, nor have we deserved them, but we ask that He would give them all to us by grace, for we daily sin much and surely deserve nothing but punishment. So we too will sincerely forgive and gladly do good to those who sin against us.

⚜ The Sixth Petition ⚜

And lead us not into temptation.

What does this mean? God tempts no one. We pray in this petition that God would guard and keep us so that the devil, the world, and our sinful nature may not deceive us or mislead us into false belief, despair, and other great shame and vice. Although we are attacked by these things, we pray that we may finally overcome them and win the victory.

✦ The Seventh Petition ✦

But deliver us from evil.

What does this mean? We pray in this petition, in summary, that our Father in heaven would rescue us from every evil of body and soul, possessions and reputation, and finally, when our last hour comes, give us a blessed end, and graciously take us from this valley of sorrow to Himself in heaven.

✦ The Conclusion ✦

For Thine is the kingdom and the power

and the glory forever and ever. Amen.

What does this mean? This means that I should be certain that these petitions are pleasing to our Father in heaven, and are heard by Him; for He Himself has commanded us to pray in this way and has promised to hear us. Amen, amen means "yes, yes, it shall be so."

The Sacrament of Holy Baptism

As the head of the family should teach it in a simple way to his household

First

What is Baptism?

Baptism is not just plain water, but it is the water included in God's command and combined with God's word.

Which is that word of God?

Christ our Lord says in the last chapter of Matthew: "Therefore go and make disciples of all nations, baptizing them in the name of the Father and of the Son and of the Holy Spirit." [Matthew 28:19]

Second

What benefits does Baptism give?

It works forgiveness of sins, rescues from death and the devil, and gives eternal salvation to all who believe this, as the words and promises of God declare.

Which are these words and promises of God?

Christ our LORD says in the last chapter of Mark: "Whoever believes and is baptized will be saved, but whoever does not believe will be condemned." [Mark 16:16]

Third

How can water do such great things?

Certainly not just water, but the word of God in and with the water does these things, along with the faith which trusts this word of God in the water. For without God's word the water is plain water and no Baptism. But with the word of God it is a Baptism, that is, a life-giving water, rich in grace, and a washing of the new birth in the Holy Spirit, as St. Paul says in Titus chapter three:

"He saved us through the washing of rebirth and renewal by the Holy Spirit, whom He poured out on us generously through Jesus Christ our Savior, so that, having been justified by His grace, we might become heirs having the hope of eternal life. This is a trustworthy saying." *[Titus 3:5–8]*

◄ Fourth ►

What does such baptizing with water indicate?

It indicates that the Old Adam in us should by daily contrition and repentance be drowned and die with all sins and evil desires, and that a new man should daily emerge and arise to live before God in righteousness and purity forever.

Where is this written?

St. Paul writes in Romans chapter six: "We were therefore buried with Him through baptism into death in order that, just as Christ was raised from the dead through the glory of the Father, we too may live a new life." [Romans 6:4]

Confession and The Office of the Keys

How Christians should be taught to confess.

What is Confession?

Confession has two parts.

First, that we confess our sins, and second, that we receive absolution, that is, forgiveness, from the pastor as from God Himself, not doubting, but firmly believing that by it our sins are forgiven before God in heaven.

What sins should we confess?

Before God we should plead guilty of all sins, even those we are not aware of, as we do in the LORD's Prayer; but before the pastor we should confess only those sins which we know and feel in our hearts.

Which are these?

Consider your place in life according to the Ten Commandments: Are you a father, mother, son, daughter, husband, wife, or worker? Have you been disobedient, unfaithful, or lazy? Have you been hot-tempered, rude, or quarrelsome? Have you hurt someone by your words or deeds? Have you stolen, been negligent, wasted anything, or done any harm?

A Short Form of Confession

[Luther intended the following form to serve only as an example of private confession for Christians of his time.]

The penitent says: Dear confessor, I ask you please to hear my confession and to pronounce forgiveness in order to fulfill God's will.

I, a poor sinner, plead guilty before God of all sins. In particular I confess before you that as a servant, maid, etc., I, sad to say, serve my master unfaithfully, for in this and that I have not done what I was told to do. I have hade him angry and caused him to curse. I have been negligent and allowed damage to be done. I have also been offensive in words and deeds. I have quarreled with my peers. I have grumbled about the lady of the house and cursed her. I am sorry for all of this and I ask for grace. I want to do better.

A master or lady of the house may say:

In particular I confess before you that I have not faithfully guided my children, servants, and wife to the glory of God. I have cursed. I have set a bad example by indecent words and deeds. I have hurt my neighbor and spoken evil of him. I have overcharged, sold inferior merchandise, and given less than was paid for.

[Let the penitent confess whatever else he has done against God's commandments and his own position.]

If, however, someone does not find himself burdened with these or greater sins, he should not trouble himself or search for or invent other sins, and thereby make confession a torture. Instead, he should mention one or two that he knows: In particular I confess that I have cursed; I have used improper words; I have neglected this or that, etc. Let that be enough.

But if you know of none at all (which hardly seems possible), then mention none in particular, but receive the forgiveness upon the general confession which you make to God before the confessor.

Then the confessor shall say:

God be merciful to you and strengthen your faith. Amen.

Furthermore:

Do you believe that my forgiveness is God's forgiveness?

Yes, dear confessor.

Then let him say:

Let it be done for you as you believe. And I, by the command of our Lord Jesus Christ, forgive you your sins in the name of the Father and of the Son and of the Holy Spirit. Amen. Go in peace.

A confessor will know additional passages with which to comfort and to strengthen the faith of those who have great burdens of conscience or are sorrowful and distressed.

This is intended only as a general form of confession.

What is the Office of the Keys?

The Office of the Keys is that special authority which Christ has given to His Church on earth to forgive the sins of repentant sinners, but to withhold forgiveness from the unrepentant as long as they do not repent.

Where is this written?

This is what St. John the Evangelist writes in chapter twenty: The Lord Jesus breathed on His disciples and said, "Receive the Holy Spirit. If you forgive anyone his sins, they are forgiven; if you do not forgive them, they are not forgiven." [John 20:22–23]

What do you believe according to these words?

I believe that when the called ministers of Christ deal with us by His divine command, in particular when they exclude openly unrepentant sinners from the Christian congregation and absolve those who repent of their sins and want to do better, this is just as valid and certain, even in heaven, as if Christ our dear Lord dealt with us Himself.

The Sacrament of the Altar

As the head of the family should teach it in a simple way to his household

What is the Sacrament of the Altar?

It is the true body and blood of our Lord Jesus Christ under the bread and wine, instituted by Christ Himself for us Christians to eat and to drink.

Where is this written?

The holy Evangelists Matthew, Mark, Luke, and St. Paul write:

Our LORD Jesus Christ, on the night when He was betrayed, took bread, and when He had given thanks, He broke it and gave it to the disciples and said: "Take, eat; this is My body, which is given for you. This do in remembrance of Me."

In the same way also He took the cup after supper, and when He had given thanks, He gave it to them, saying, "Drink of it, all of you; this cup is the new testament in My blood, which is shed for you for the forgiveness of sins. This do, as often as you drink it, in remembrance of Me."

What is the benefit of this eating and drinking?

These words, "Given and shed for you for the forgiveness of sins," show us that in the Sacrament forgiveness of sins, life, and salvation are given us through these words. For where there is forgiveness of sins, there is also life and salvation.

How can bodily eating and drinking do such great things?

Certainly not just eating and drinking do these things, but the words written here: "Given and shed for you for the forgiveness of sins." These words, along with the bodily eating and drinking, are the main thing in the Sacrament. Whoever believes these words has exactly what they say: "forgiveness of sins."

Who receives this sacrament worthily?

Fasting and bodily preparation are certainly fine outward training. But that person is truly worthy and well prepared who has faith in these words: "Given and shed for you for the forgiveness of sins."

But anyone who does not believe these words or doubts them is unworthy and unprepared, for the words "for you" require all hearts to believe.

Daily Prayers

How the head of the family should teach his household to pray morning and evening

⸺ Morning Prayer ⸺

In the morning when you get up, make the sign of the holy cross and say:

In the name of the Father and of the ✠ Son and of the Holy Spirit. Amen.

Then, kneeling or standing, repeat the Creed and the Lord's Prayer. If you choose, you may also say this little prayer:

I thank You, my heavenly Father, through Jesus Christ, Your dear Son, that You have kept me this night from all harm and danger; and I pray that You would keep me this day also from sin and every evil, that all my doings and life may please You. For into Your hands I commend myself, my body and soul, and all things. Let Your holy angel be with me, that the evil foe may have no power over me. Amen.

Then go joyfully to your work, singing a hymn, like that of the Ten Commandments, or whatever your devotion may suggest.

⸺ Evening Prayer ⸺

In the evening when you go to bed, make the sign of the holy cross and say:

In the name of the Father and of the ✠ Son and of the Holy Spirit. Amen.

Then kneeling or standing, repeat the Creed and the Lord's Prayer. If you choose, you may also say this little prayer:

I thank You, my heavenly Father, through Jesus Christ, Your dear Son, that You have graciously kept me this day; and I pray that You would forgive me all my sins where I have done wrong, and graciously keep me this night. For into Your hands I commend myself, my body and soul, and all things. Let Your holy angel be with me, that the evil foe may have no power over me. Amen.

Then go to sleep at once and in good cheer.

How the head of the family should teach his household to ask a blessing and return thanks

Asking a Blessing

The children and the members of the household shall go the table reverently, fold their hands, and say:

The eyes of all look to You, O Lord, and You give them their food at the proper time. You open your hand and satisfy the desires of every living thing. *[Psalm 145:15–16]*

Then shall be said the Lord's Prayer and the following:

Lord God, heavenly Father, bless us and these Your gifts which we receive from Your bountiful goodness, through Jesus Christ, our Lord. Amen.

Returning Thanks

Also, after eating, they shall, in like manner, reverently and with folded hands say:

Give thanks to the Lord, for He is good, His love endures forever. He gives food to every creature. He provides food for the cattle and for the young ravens when they call. His pleasure is not in the strength of the horse, nor His delight in the legs of a man; the Lord delights in those who fear Him, who put their hope in His unfailing love. [Psalm 136:1, 25; 147:9–11]

Then shall be said the Lord's Prayer and the following:

We thank You, Lord God, heavenly Father, for all Your benefits, through Jesus Christ, our Lord, who lives and reigns with You and the Holy Spirit forever and ever. Amen.

Table of Duties

Certain passages of Scripture for various holy orders and positions, admonishing them about their duties and responsibilities

To Bishops, Pastors, and Preachers

The overseer must be above reproach, the husband of but one wife, temperate, self-controlled, respectable, hospitable, able to teach, not given to drunkenness, not violent but gentle, not quarrelsome, not a lover of money. He must manage his own family well and see that his children obey him with proper respect. *1 Timothy 3:2–4*

He must not be a recent convert, or he may become conceited and fall under the same judgment as the devil. *1 Timothy 3:6*

He must hold firmly to the trustworthy message as it has been taught, so that he can encourage others by sound doctrine and refute those who oppose it. *Titus 1:9*

What the Hearers Owe Their Pastors

The Lord has commanded that those who preach the gospel should receive their living from the gospel. *1 Corinthians 9:14*

Anyone who receives instruction in the word must share all good things with his instructor. Do not be deceived: God cannot be mocked. A man reaps what he sows. *Galatians 6:6–7*

The elders who direct the affairs of the church

well are worthy of double honor, especially those whose work is preaching and teaching. For the Scripture says, "Do not muzzle the ox while it is treading out the grain," and "The worker deserves his wages." *1 Timothy 5:17–18*

We ask you, brothers, to respect those who work hard among you, who are over you in the Lord and who admonish you. Hold them in the highest regard in love because of their work. Live in peace with each other. *1 Thessalonians 5:12–13*

Obey your leaders and submit to their authority. They keep watch over you as men who must give an account. Obey them so that their work will be a joy, not a burden, for that would be of no advantage to you. *Hebrews 13:17*

Of Civil Government

Everyone must submit himself to the governing authorities, for there is no authority except that which God has established. The authorities that exist have been established by God. Consequently, he who rebels against the authority is rebelling against what God has instituted, and those who do so will bring judgment on themselves. For rulers hold no terror for those who do right, but for those who do wrong. Do you want to be free from fear of the one in authority?

Then do what is right and he will commend you. For he is God's servant to do you good. But if you do wrong, be afraid, for he does not bear the sword for nothing. He is God's servant, an agent of wrath to bring punishment on the wrongdoer. *Romans 13:1–4*

Of Citizens

Give to Caesar what is Caesar's, and to God what is God's. *Matthew 22:21*

It is necessary to submit to the authorities, not only because of possible punishment but also because of conscience. This is also why you pay taxes, for the authorities are God's servants, who give their full time to governing. Give everyone what you owe him: If you owe taxes, pay taxes; if revenue, then revenue; if respect, then respect; if honor, then honor. *Romans 13:5–7*

I urge, then, first of all, that requests, prayers, intercession and thanksgiving be made for everyone—for kings and all those in authority, that we may live peaceful and quiet lives in all godliness and holiness. This is good, and pleases God our Savior. *1 Timothy 2:1–3*

Remind the people to be subject to rulers and authorities, to be obedient, to be ready to do whatever is good. *Titus 3:1*

Submit yourselves for the Lord's sake to every authority instituted among men: whether to the king, as the supreme authority, or to governors, who are sent by him to punish those who do wrong and to commend those who do right. *1 Peter 2:13–14*

___ To Husbands ___

Husbands, in the same way be considerate as you live with your wives, and treat them with respect as the weaker partner and as heirs with you of the gracious gift of life, so that nothing will hinder your prayers. *1 Peter 3:7*

Husbands, love your wives and do not be harsh with them. *Colossians 3:19*

___ To Wives ___

Wives, submit to your husbands as to the Lord. *Ephesians 5:22*

They were submissive to their own husbands, like Sarah, who obeyed Abraham and called him her master. You are her daughters if you do what is right and do not give way to fear. *1 Peter 3:5–6*

To Parents

Fathers, do not exasperate your children; instead, bring them up in the training and instruction of the Lord.

Ephesians 6:4

To Children

Children, obey your parents in the Lord, for this is right. "Honor your father and your mother"—which is the first commandment with a promise—"that it may go well with you and that you may enjoy long life on the earth."

Ephesians 6:1–3

To Workers of All Kinds

Slaves, obey your earthly masters with respect and fear, and with sincerity of heart, just as you would obey Christ. Obey them not only to win their favor when their eye is on you, but like slaves of Christ, doing the will of God from your heart. Serve wholeheartedly, as if you were serving the Lord, not men, because you know that the Lord will reward everyone for whatever good he does, whether he is slave or free.

Ephesians 6:5–8

To Employers and Supervisors

Masters, treat your slaves in the same way. Do not threaten them, since you know that he who is both their Master and yours is in heaven, and there is no favoritism with Him. *Ephesians 6:9*

To Youth

Young men, in the same way be submissive to those who are older. All of you, clothe yourselves with humility toward one another, because, "God opposes the proud but gives grace to the humble." Humble yourselves, therefore, under God's mighty hand, that He may lift you up in due time.

1 Peter 5:5–6

To Widows

The widow who is really in need and left all alone puts her hope in God and continues night and day to pray and to ask God for help. But the widow who lives for pleasure is dead even while she lives.

1 Timothy 5:5–6

To Everyone

The commandments . . . are summed up in

this one rule: "Love your neighbor as yourself."

Romans 13:9

I urge . . . that requests, prayers, intercession and thanksgiving be made for everyone.

1 Timothy 2:1

Let each his lesson learn with care,
And all the household well shall fare.

Scripture quotations are taken from The Holy Bible, English Standard Version, copyright © 2001 by Crossway Bibles, a division of Good News Publishers. Used by permission. All rights reserved.

Orders for Daily Prayer from *The Hymnal Supplement 98* © 1998 Concordia Publishing House (pp 28–32,) as revised for the Lutheran Hymnal Project © 2003 The Lutheran Church—Missouri Synod. Unless otherwise indicated, Scripture quotations for the orders are from the HOLY BIBLE NEW INTERNATIONAL VERSION®. Copyright © 1973, 1978, 1984 by the International Bible Society. Used by permission of Zondervan Publishing House.

The hymn marked with the abbreviation *LW* is from *Lutheran Worship*, copyright © 1982 Concordia Publishing House.

The hymn marked with the abbreviation *LBW* is from *Lutheran Book Of Worship*, copyright © 1978. Copyright administered by Augsburg Fortress Publishers and Concordia Publishing House. Used by permission.

Canticles and prayers, unless otherwise indicated, are from *Lutheran Worship Altar Book* and/or *Lutheran Worship Agenda,* copyright © 1984 Concordia Publishing House.

Prayers numbered 1, 15, 16, 17, 18, 25, 26, 28, 29, 30, 33, 38, and 42 are adapted from *The Daily Office,* Herbert Lindemann, editor; copyright © 1965 Concordia Publishing House. All rights reserved

Prayers numbered 2, 3, 4, 5, 6, 7, 8, 9, 10, 11, 12, 13, and 14 are taken from *Lutheran Worship,* copyright © 1982 Concordia Publishing House.

Prayers numbered 19, 23, 24, 27, 32, and 39 are taken from *Lutheran Worship Altar Book,* copyright © 1984 Concordia Publishing House.

Prayers numbered 21, 31, 34, 35, and 36 are taken from *Lutheran Worship Agenda,* copyright © 1984 Concordia Publishing House.

Prayer 41 is taken from *The Lutheran Hymnal,* copyright © 1941 Concordia Publishing House.

Prayer 43 is taken from *The Lutheran Liturgy,* copyright © Concordia Publishing House.

Summary of Christian Faith quotations are from *Luther's Small Catechism with Explanation,* copyright © 1991 Concordia Publishing House. All rights reserved.

Manufactured in the United States of America

1 2 3 4 5 6 7 8 9 10   13 12 11 10 09 08 07 06 05 04